An English Prayer Book

An English
PRAYER BOOK

OXFORD UNIVERSITY PRESS

Interpretation

No doctrine or practices may be construed or based on the revised services, apart from those authorized by the 39 Articles of Religion and/or the *Book of Common Prayer* of 1662.

CHURCH SOCIETY

Dean Wace House, 16 Rosslyn Road, Watford WD1 7EY

Registered Charity 249574

Oxford University Press, Great Clarendon Street, Oxford OX2 6DP
Oxford New York
Athens Auckland Bangkok Bogotá Buenos Aires Calcutta
Cape Town Chennai Dar es Salaam Delhi Florence Hong Kong Istanbul
Karachi Kuala Lumpur Madrid Melbourne Mexico City Mumbai
Nairobi Paris São Paulo Singapore Taipei Tokyo Toronto Warsaw
and associated companies in
Berlin Ibadan

Oxford is a registered trade mark of Oxford University Press

Published in the United States by
Oxford University Press Inc., New York

British Library Cataloguing in Publication Data
Data available

Library of Congress Cataloging in Publication Data
Data available
ISBN 0-19-110010-2

10 9 8 7 6 5 4 3 2

Printed in Great Britain
on acid-free paper by
Butler & Tanner Ltd., Frome, Somerset

Contents

Preface

by Roger Beckwith, Warden of Latimer House

An English Prayer Book is an unofficial but (its compilers hope) a constructive contribution to the revision of the *Alternative Service Book 1980*, a revision which is scheduled to take place in the year 2000. The Liturgical Commission, which has the responsibility of making official proposals about revision, has been giving somewhat conflicting signals as to how it thinks this work should be done. In its reports *Lent, Holy Week, Easter* (1986) and *The Promise of his Glory* (1990) it seemed to feel free to move a further stage away from traditional Anglican worship, beyond what its predecessors had done in producing the *ASB*, and in its report *Patterns for Worship* (1989) it even seemed to be moving away from liturgical worship altogether. Again, in its report *The Worship of the Church* (1991) it spoke of the possibility of replacing the *ASB* by a range of books rather than by a single book (shades of the Middle Ages!), and, at the same time, of making concessions to various fashionable cults of the day. On the other hand, in its more recent report *The Renewal of Common Prayer* (1993), it has clearly acknowledged the Anglican ideal of common prayer, or prayer for use by everybody, and the important place of the *Book of Common Prayer* (1662) in maintaining or restoring it. This is a trend in the Commission's thinking which the compilers of the present work would like to encourage.

The *Alternative Service Book 1980*, as its title indicates, was intended as an alternative and not as a replacement to the 1662 Prayer Book. The latter remains the permanent, official standard of Anglican worship, as the Worship and Doctrine Measure of 1974 (now the legal basis of Anglican worship) makes quite clear. The Measure adds that the *Book of Common Prayer*, alongside the Creeds which it contains and the 39 Articles which are appended to it, is one of the standards of Anglican doctrine, subject only to Holy Scripture itself. Alternative services should conform to these norms, but are not norms themselves.

One day the Church of England may come back to the question of revising the 1662 Prayer Book, but that lies well in the future. If the Church does, it will have to give careful attention to the cautious principles for liturgical revision laid down in its own Preface, which are designed to ensure that, with any necessary updating, the book remains recognizably the same, still reflecting the liturgical mastery of Cranmer and grounded on the pure teaching of the Bible. But that is also a task for another day. At present, we are concerned with revising the *ASB*.

The *Alternative Service Book 1980* was the culmination of a process of liturgical revision beginning soon after the Second World War, in which the first publication was the Liturgical Commission's report *Prayer Book Revision in the Church of England* (1957). It was followed by three series of Alternative Services, in paperback and pamphlet form (the third of the series being in a modern idiom of English), and then by the *ASB*, which combined a selection of the services into a bound volume. Remarkably enough, the principles on which the Liturgical Commission worked in producing this report and these series of services were not the same as those embodied in the legislation (drawn up by the Church Assembly and General Synod) which afterwards authorized the services for use. The Commission told us that it wished to set the *Book of*

Common Prayer aside as a standard for worship and a starting point for revision, and that in matters of doctrine it wished to pursue 'studied ambiguity'. The greatest opportunity which the coming revision of the *ASB* offers is to introduce consistency into the liturgical process, by recognizing that the *ASB*, though different from the Prayer Book, *must* conform to the doctrine of the Prayer Book, and that in liturgical matters it ought to show due regard to the fact that the Prayer Book will continue in use, and continue to be the standard. It is hoped that the present Liturgical Commission, with its quite altered membership, will be willing to reopen these basic questions, and to give different answers to them from those given by its predecessors.

An English Prayer Book aims to show, in practical terms, what such a change of policy might mean. Though using the modern language of the *ASB*, and including many detailed features of the *ASB*, where these have proved valuable, it aims throughout to give clear expression to the doctrine of the Prayer Book and to show proper respect to its liturgical usages. It restores the doctrinal items which are conspicuously absent from the *ASB* (the Catechism, the 39 Articles and the Athanasian Creed), it conforms to the calendar of the Prayer Book and to its incomparable set of collects, and in many other respects it attempts to bring the *ASB* closer to the Prayer Book, where there had been no adequate reason for moving away.

We recognize that there is a widespread desire for services in modern English that adhere to the biblical teaching of the Prayer Book (a desire which the *ASB* has excited but not fulfilled). We earnestly hope that our work will be accepted as a worthwhile contribution to the forthcoming revision of the *ASB*.

Finally, the compilers would like to acknowledge their consciousness that many faults may be found in their work: they express their hope that nevertheless it may be accepted by Almighty God, and in a small way that it may bring glory to him and edification to his church and people.

An English Prayer Book

Use of Italics
Italics are used in places where plural words or expressions may be substituted for singular (or vice versa), or feminine for masculine.

Scripture Sentences

for use at the beginning of services

God is our refuge and strength, an ever-present help in trouble.
Psalm 46: 1

I know my transgressions, and my sin is always before me.
Psalm 51: 3

Hide your face from my sins and blot out all my iniquity.
Psalm 51: 9

The sacrifices of God are a broken spirit; a broken and contrite
heart, O God, you will not despise. *Psalm 51: 17*

This is the day the Lord has made; let us rejoice and be glad in it.
Psalm 118: 24

Do not bring your servant into judgement, for no one living is
righteous before you. *Psalm 143: 2*

Seek the Lord while he may be found; call on him while he is
near. *Isaiah 55: 6*

Correct me, Lord, but only with justice—not in your anger, lest
you reduce me to nothing. *Jeremiah 10: 24*

If a wicked man turns away from the wickedness he has
committed and does what is just and right, he will save his life.
Ezekiel 18: 27

The Lord our God is merciful and forgiving, even though we
have rebelled against him; we have not obeyed the Lord our God
or kept the laws he gave us. *Daniel 9: 9 f.*

Rend your heart and not your garments. Return to the Lord your God, for he is gracious and compassionate, slow to anger, and abounding in love. *Joel 2: 13*

The Lord is in his holy temple; let all the earth be silent before him. *Habakkuk 2: 20*

Repent for the kingdom of heaven is near. *Matthew 3: 2*

I will set out and go back to my father and say to him: Father I have sinned against heaven and against you. I am no longer worthy to be called your son. *Luke 15: 18 f.*

A time is coming and has now come when the true worshippers will worship the Father in spirit and truth, for they are the kind of worshippers the Father seeks. God is spirit and his worshippers must worship in spirit and truth. *John 4: 23 f.*

Do not be anxious about anything, but in everything, by prayer and petition, with thanksgiving, present your requests to God. *Philippians 4: 6*

Through Jesus, therefore, let us continually offer to God a sacrifice of praise—the fruit of lips that confess his name. *Hebrews 13: 15*

If we claim to be without sin, we deceive ourselves and the truth is not in us. If we confess our sins, he is faithful and just and will forgive us our sins and purify us from all unrighteousness. *1 John 1: 8 f.*

You are worthy, our Lord and God, to receive glory and honour and power, for you created all things, and by your will they were created and have their being. *Revelation 4: 11*

Christmas

For to us a child is born, to us a son is given, and the government will be upon his shoulders. And he will be called Wonderful Counsellor, Mighty God, Everlasting Father, Prince of Peace. *Isaiah 9: 6*

When the time had fully come, God sent his Son, born of a woman, born under law, to redeem those under law, that we might receive the full rights of sons. *Galatians 4: 4*

This is how God showed his love among us: He sent his one and only Son into the world that we might live through him. *1 John 4: 9*

Easter

For Christ our Passover lamb, has been sacrificed. Therefore let us keep the Festival, not with the old yeast, the yeast of malice and wickedness, but with bread without yeast, the bread of sincerity and truth. *1 Corinthians 5: 7 f.*

Praise be to the God and Father of our Lord Jesus Christ! In his great mercy he has given us new birth into a living hope through the resurrection of Jesus Christ from the dead. *1 Peter 1: 3*

Ascension

God exalted Christ to the highest place and gave him the name that is above every name, that at the name of Jesus every knee should bow, in heaven and on earth and under the earth, and every tongue confess that Jesus Christ is Lord, to the glory of God the Father. *Philippians 2: 9–11*

Whitsun (Pentecost)

You will receive power when the Holy Spirit comes on you; and you will be my witnesses. *Acts 1: 8*

God has poured out his love into our hearts by the Holy Spirit, whom he has given us. *Romans 5: 5*

Trinity

Day and night those around the throne never stop saying: 'Holy, holy, holy is the Lord God Almighty, who was, and is, and is to come.' *Revelation 4: 8*

Morning and Evening Prayer

1   *The minister welcomes the people and announces the
     opening* HYMN.

2   *The minister reads one or more* SCRIPTURE SENTENCES
     and then says these WORDS OF EXHORTATION:

either

The Bible encourages us repeatedly to acknowledge
and confess our many sins and evil ways and that we
should not try to hide them from Almighty God our
heavenly Father. We are to confess them with a
humble, lowly, penitent, and obedient heart so that
we may receive forgiveness through God's infinite
goodness and mercy.

   We should humbly admit our sins to God at all
times, but especially when we come together to give
thanks for the blessings we have received from him, to
offer the praise that is his due, to hear his most holy
Word, to ask him to supply all our needs, and to pray
for others as well as ourselves.

   Let us then with a pure heart and humble voice
approach our Father's throne of grace, and pray together:

or

We have come together in our Father's presence to
offer him, through our Lord Jesus Christ, praise and
thanksgiving; to hear his most holy Word; to pray for
others as well as ourselves; and to ask forgiveness for
our sins. Let us then confess our sins to Almighty God
and pray together:

3   CONFESSION:

either

All   Almighty and most merciful Father,
we have erred and strayed from your ways like lost
     sheep.
We have followed too much the devices
and desires of our own hearts.
We have broken your holy laws.
We have left undone what we ought to have done,
     and
we have done what we ought not to have done.
O Lord, have mercy on us pitiful sinners.
Spare those, O God, who confess their faults.
Restore those who truly repent,
as you have promised through Jesus Christ our Lord.
And grant, O merciful Father, for his sake,
that we may live a godly, righteous, and disciplined
     life,
to the praise of your holy name. Amen.

or

Most merciful Father, our Creator and Judge,
we acknowledge and confess
that we have sinned against you
in thought, word, and deed.
We have not loved you with all our heart;
and we have not loved our neighbours as ourselves.
We earnestly repent,
and are truly sorry for all our sins.
For your Son our Lord Jesus Christ's sake forgive us,
and strengthen us to serve and obey you
in lives wholly renewed by your Spirit;
through Jesus Christ our Lord. Amen.

4   *The minister declares* GOD'S FORGIVENESS, *saying:*

either

Almighty God, the Father of our Lord Jesus Christ, does
not desire the death of sinners but rather that they
should turn from their wickedness and live. He has
commanded and authorized his ministers to reassure
his people that they will be forgiven when they repent
of their sins. God pardons and forgives all who truly
repent and sincerely believe his holy gospel. Therefore
let us beseech him to grant us true repentance and his
Holy Spirit; so that what we do now may please him,
that the rest of our lives may be pure and holy, and
that finally we may come to his eternal joy; through
Jesus Christ our Lord. **Amen.**

or

Loving Father we rejoice that you pardon and forgive
all those who truly repent and sincerely believe your
holy gospel: grant us true repentance and your holy
Spirit; so that we may live godly, righteous and holy
lives and that we may come at the last to your eternal
glory; through Jesus Christ our Lord. **Amen.**

or

Merciful God, grant to your faithful people pardon and
peace; that we may be cleansed from all our sins and
serve you with a quiet mind; through Jesus Christ our
Lord. **Amen.**

5   THE LORD'S PRAYER:

either	*or*
All **Our Father who art in heaven,**	**Our Father in heaven, hallowed be your name,**

19

hallowed be thy name,
thy kingdom come,
thy will be done,
on earth as it is in heaven.
Give us this day
our daily bread.
And forgive us our
    trespasses
as we forgive those
who trespass against us.
And lead us not into
    temptation
but deliver us from evil.
For thine is the kingdom,
the power, and the glory,
for ever and ever. Amen.

your kingdom come,
your will be done,
on earth as it is in heaven.
Give us today
our daily bread.
Forgive us our sins
as we forgive those
who sin against us.
Lead us not into
    temptation
but deliver us from evil.
For yours is the kingdom,
the power, and the glory,
now and for ever. Amen.

6   RESPONSES

Minister   Open our lips, O Lord.
People   **And we shall declare your praise.**

Minister   O God, make speed to save us.
People   **O Lord, make haste to help us.**

Minister   Glory be to the Father, and to the Son,
           and to the Holy Spirit:
People   **as it was in the beginning, is now,
           and shall be for ever. Amen.**

Minister   Let us praise the Lord.
People   **The Lord's name be praised.**

7   A PSALM, *or Psalms, is said or sung.*

8   THE SCRIPTURE READINGS

*A psalm, hymn, or canticle may be said or sung between the
readings from the Old and New Testaments. A period of silence
may follow the response after each reading.*

After each reading the reader says:

This is the word of the Lord.

All   **Thanks be to God.**

9   *The* NOTICES *and* BANNS OF MARRIAGE *may be
announced, after which the* OFFERING *is brought forward
and received.*

10   A PSALM, HYMN, *or* CANTICLE *may be said or sung.*

11   THE APOSTLES' CREED

All   **I believe in God, the Father Almighty,
Creator of heaven and earth.**

     **I believe in Jesus Christ,
his only Son, our Lord.
He was conceived by the Holy Spirit
and born of the virgin Mary.
He suffered under Pontius Pilate,
was crucified, died, and was buried.
He descended to the dead.
On the third day he rose again.
He ascended into heaven,
and sits at the right hand of the Father.
From there he shall come again
to judge the living and the dead.**

I believe in the Holy Spirit,
the holy catholic church,
the communion of saints,
the forgiveness of sins,
the resurrection of the body,
and the life everlasting. Amen.

12   THE RESPONSES

Minister   The Lord be with you.
People   **And with your spirit.**
Minister   Let us pray.

Minister   O Lord, show us your mercy,
People   **and grant us your salvation.**
Minister   O Lord, save the *Queen,*
People   **and mercifully hear us when we pray to you.**
Minister   Endow your ministers with righteousness,
People   **and make your chosen people joyful.**
Minister   O Lord, save your people,
People   **and bless your inheritance.**
Minister   Give peace in our time, O Lord,
People   **for you are our help and strength.**
Minister   O God, cleanse our hearts,
People   **and revive us by your Holy Spirit.**

13   THE COLLECT *(special prayer)* OF THE DAY *(pp. 84 ff.)*

14   *At MORNING PRAYER one or both of these prayers are used:*

All   **O Lord our heavenly Father,**
        Almighty and everlasting God,
        we praise you for bringing us safely

to the beginning of this day:
defend us with your mighty power,
and grant that we fall into no sin,
nor run into any kind of danger,
but govern and guide us at all times,
so that we may do what is right in your sight;
through Jesus Christ our Lord. Amen.

O God, the author and lover of peace,
whom to know is eternal life
and to serve is perfect freedom:
defend us your humble servants
against all assaults of our enemies,
that trusting in your defence,
we may not fear the power of any adversary;
through the might of Jesus Christ our Lord. Amen.

At EVENING PRAYER *one or both of these prayers are used:*

All   O God, the author of all holy desires,
all good purposes, and all just works:
give to us your servants that peace
which the world cannot give,
so that we, obeying your commands,
and being delivered from the fear of our enemies,
may live in rest and quietness;
through the merits of Jesus Christ our Saviour. Amen.

Lighten our darkness, Lord:
and by your great mercy defend us
from all peril and danger this night;
for the love of your only Son
our Saviour Jesus Christ. Amen.

15   A HYMN *or* ANTHEM *may be sung.*

16   *Other* PRAYERS, *including remembrance of the monarch and royal family (see e.g. pp. 39 ff). These may end with* THE GRACE.

All   **The grace of our Lord Jesus Christ,**
         and the love of God,
         and the fellowship of the Holy Spirit,
         be with us all evermore. Amen.

17   *On Sundays the service may continue with the* NOTICES *(if not announced at section 9) and a* HYMN *is sung.*

18   THE SERMON *is preached.*

19   *A concluding* HYMN *is sung and then the minister dismisses the people with a* PRAYER *or* BLESSING.

     These BLESSINGS *may be used:*

The Lord bless you and keep you; the Lord make his face to shine upon you and be gracious to you; the Lord turn his face towards you and give you his peace; through Jesus Christ our Lord. **Amen.**

The peace of God which passes all understanding, keep your hearts and minds in the knowledge and love of God, and of his Son Jesus Christ our Lord; and the blessing of God Almighty, the Father, the Son, and the Holy Spirit, be upon you and remain with you always. **Amen.**

24

Canticles

1 PSALM 67 (*Deus misereatur*)

May God be gracious to ⏐ us and ⏐ bless us
and make his ⏐ face ⏐ shine up⏐on us,

that your ways may be ⏐ known on ⏐ earth,
your sal⏐vation a⏐mong all ⏐ nations.

May the peoples ⏐ praise · you O ⏐ God;
may ⏐ all the ⏐ peoples ⏐ praise you.

May the nations be glad and ⏐ sing for ⏐ joy,
for you rule the peoples justly *
and guide the ⏐ nations ⏐ of the ⏐ earth.

May the peoples ⏐ praise · you O ⏐ God;
may ⏐ all the ⏐ peoples ⏐ praise you.

Then the land will ⏐ yield its ⏐ harvest,
and ⏐ God, our ⏐ God, will ⏐ bless us.

God ⏐ will ⏐ bless us,
and all the ⏐ ends · of the ⏐ earth will ⏐ fear him.

2 PSALM 95 (*Venite*)

Come let us sing for ⏐ joy · to the ⏐ Lord;
let us shout aloud to the ⏐ Rock of ⏐ our sal⏐vation.

Let us come be'fore him · with ˈ thanksgiving
and ex'tol him · with ˈ music · and ˈ song.

For the Lord is the ˈ great ˈ God,
the great ˈ King a'bove all ˈ gods.

In his hands are the ˈ depths of · the ˈ earth,
and the mountain ˈ peaks be'long to ˈ him.

The sea is ˈ his for · he ˈ made it,
and his hands ˈ formed the ˈ dry ˈ land.

Come let us bow ˈ down in ˈ worship,
let us kneel be'fore the ˈ Lord our ˈ Maker;

for he ˈ is our ˈ God
and we are the people of his pasture, *
the ˈ flock ˈ under · his ˈ care.

Today if you ˈ hear his ˈ voice,
do not harden your hearts as you did at Meribah, *
as you did that day at ˈ Massah ˈ in the ˈ desert,

where your fathers ˈ tested · and ˈ tried me,
though they had ˈ seen ˈ what I ˈ did.

For forty years I was angry with that ˈ gener'ation;
I said, * 'They are a people whose hearts go astray, *
and they ˈ have not ˈ known my ˈ ways.'

So I declared on ˈ oath · in my ˈ anger,
'They shall ˈ never ˈ enter · my ˈ rest.'

3   PSALM 98 (*Cantate Domino*)

Sing to the Lord a ' new ' song:
for ' he has · done ' marvel · lous ' things;

his right hand and his ' holy ' arm
have ' worked sal'vation ' for him.

The Lord has made his sal'vation ' known:
and revealed his ' righteous · ness ' to the ' nations.

He has remembered his love * and his faithfulness to
    the ' house of ' Israel:
all the ends of the earth have seen the sal'vation ' of
    our ' God.

Shout with joy to the ' Lord · all the ' earth:
burst into ' jubil · ant ' song with ' music;

make music to the ' Lord · with the ' harp
with trumpets and the blast of the ram's horn *
shout for joy be'fore the ' Lord the ' King.

Let the sea resound and ' every · thing ' in it:
the world and ' all who ' live ' in it.

Let the rivers clap their hands *
let the mountains sing to'gether · for ' joy:
for he ' comes to ' judge the ' earth.

He will judge the ' world in ' righteousness
and the ' peoples ' with ' equity.

CANTICLES

4   PSALM 100 (*Jubilate*)

Shout for joy to the Lord ˈ all the ˈ earth.
Worship the Lord with gladness; *
come beˈfore him · with ˈ joyful ˈ songs.

Know that the ˈ Lord is ˈ God.
It is he who made us and we are his; *
we are his ˈ people · the ˈ sheep of · his ˈ pasture.

Enter his gates with thanksgiving *
and his ˈ courts with ˈ praise;
give thanks to ˈ him and ˈ praise his ˈ name.

For the Lord is good and his love enˈdures for ˈ ever;
his faithfulness conˈtinues · through ˈ all · generˈations.

5   SONG OF ZECHARIAH (*Benedictus*)

Praise be to the Lord the ˈ God of ˈ Israel,
because he has come and ˈ has reˈdeemed his ˈ people.

He has raised up a horn of salvation for us *
in the house of his ˈ servant ˈ David,
as he said through his holy ˈ prophets · of ˈ long aˈgo,

salvation ˈ from our ˈ enemies
and from the ˈ hand of ˈ all who ˈ hate us

to show ˈ mercy · to our ˈ fathers
and to reˈmember · his ˈ holy ˈ covenant,

the oath he swore to our ˈ father ˈ Abraham:
to rescue us ˈ from the ˈ hand of · our ˈ enemies,

and to enable us to serve him with|out | fear
in holiness and righteousness be|fore him | all our | days.

And you my child will be called a prophet of
the | Most | High;
for you will go on before the Lord to pre|pare the | way
for | him,

to give his people the | knowledge of · sal|vation
through the for|giveness | of their | sins,

because of the tender mercy | of our | God,
by which the rising sun will | come to | us from | heaven

to shine on those living in darkness and in the |
shadow · of | death,
to guide our | feet in·to the | path of | peace.

6   SONG OF MARY (*Magnificat*)

My soul | glorifies · the | Lord
and my spirit re|joices · in | God my | Saviour,

for | he has · been | mindful ⌣
of the | humble | state · of his | servant.

From now on all generations will | call me | blessèd,
for the Mighty One has done great things for me *
| holy | is his | name.

His mercy extends to | those who | fear him,
from gener|ation · to | gener|ation.

He has performed mighty ' deeds · with his ' arm;
he has scattered those who are proud ' in
    their ' inmost ' thoughts.

He has brought down ' rulers · from their ' thrones
but has ' lifted ' up the ' humble.

He has filled the ' hungry · with ' good things
but has sent the ' rich a'way ' empty.

He has helped his ' servant ' Israel,
re'member·ing ' to be ' merciful

to Abraham and his de'scendants · for ' ever,
even as he ' said ' to our ' fathers.

7   SONG OF SIMEON (*Nunc dimittis*)

Sovereign Lord as ' you have ' promised,
you now dis'miss your ' servant · in ' peace.

For my eyes have ' seen · your sal'vation,
which you have ' prepared · in the ' sight · of all ' people,

a light for reve'lation · to the ' Gentiles
and for ' glory · to your ' people ' Israel.

8   THE EASTER ANTHEMS

Christ our Passover has been ' sacri·ficed ' for us:
so let us ' cele'brate the ' feast,

not with the old leaven of cor'ruption · and '
    wickedness:

but with the unleavened bread of sin⎸ceri⎸ty and
    truth.

Christ once raised from the dead ⎸ dies no ⎸ more:
death has no ⎸ more do⎸minion ⎸ over him.

In dying he died to sin ⎸ once for ⎸ all:
in ⎸ living · he ⎸ lives to ⎸ God.

See yourselves therefore as ⎸ dead to ⎸ sin:
and alive to God in ⎸ Jesus ⎸ Christ our ⎸ Lord.

Christ has been ⎸ raised · from the ⎸ dead:
the ⎸ firstfruits · of ⎸ those who ⎸ sleep.

For as by ⎸ man came ⎸ death:
by man has come also the resur⎸rection ⎸ of the ⎸ dead;

for as in ⎸ Adam · all ⎸ die:
even so in Christ shall ⎸ all be ⎸ made a⎸live.

9   A SONG OF CREATION

Bless the Lord all cre⎸ated ⎸ things:
sing his ⎸ praise · and ex⎸alt him · for ⎸ ever.

Bless the ⎸ Lord you ⎸ heavens:
sing his ⎸ praise · and ex⎸alt him · for ⎸ ever.

Bless the Lord you ⎸ angels · of the ⎸ Lord:
bless the ⎸ Lord all ⎸ you his ⎸ hosts;

bless the Lord you waters a⎸bove the ⎸ heavens:
sing his ⎸ praise · and ex⎸alt him · for ⎸ ever.

Bless the Lord ' sun and ' moon:
bless the ' Lord you ' powers of ' heaven;

bless the Lord all ' rain and ' dew:
sing his ' praise · and ex'alt him · for ' ever.

Bless the Lord all ' winds that ' blow:
bless the Lord you ' fire and ' heat;

bless the Lord scorching wind and ' bitter ' cold:
sing his ' praise · and ex'alt him · for ' ever.

Bless the Lord dews and ' falling ' snows:
bless the ' Lord you ' nights and ' days;

bless the Lord ' light and ' darkness:
sing his ' praise · and ex'alt him · for ' ever.

Bless the Lord ' frost and ' cold:
bless the ' Lord you ' ice and ' snow;

bless the Lord ' lightnings · and ' clouds:
sing his ' praise · and ex'alt him · for ' ever.

O let the earth ' bless the ' Lord:
bless the ' Lord you ' mountains · and ' hills;

bless the Lord all that ' grows · in the ' ground:
sing his ' praise · and ex'alt him · for ' ever.

Bless the ' Lord you · springs:
bless the ' Lord you ' seas and ' rivers;

bless the Lord you whales and all that ' swim · in the '
   waters:
sing his ' praise · and ex'alt him · for ' ever.

Bless the Lord all ' birds · of the ' air:
bless the ' Lord you ' beasts and ' cattle;

bless the Lord all ' men · on the ' earth:
sing his ' praise · and ex'alt him · for ' ever.

O people of God ' bless the ' Lord:
bless the ' Lord you ' priests · of the ' Lord;

bless the Lord you ' servants · of the ' Lord:
sing his ' praise · and ex'alt him · for ' ever.

Bless the Lord all men of ' upright ' spirit:
bless the Lord you that are ' holy · and ' humble · in '
   heart.

Bless the Father the Son and the ' Holy ' Spirit:
sing his ' praise · and ex'alt him · for ' ever.

10   GREAT AND WONDERFUL

Great and wonderful are your deeds Lord ' God · the
   Al'mighty:
just and true are your ' ways O ' King · of the ' nations.

Who shall not revere and praise your ' name O ' Lord?
for ' you a'lone are ' holy.

All nations shall come and worship ' in your ' presence:
for your just ' dealings · have ' been re'vealed.

33

To him who sits on the throne and ˡ to the ˡ Lamb:
be praise and honour, glory and might for ever and ˡ
    ever. ˡ Aˡmen.

11   TE DEUM

You are ˡ God · and we ˡ praise you:
you are the ˡ Lord and ˡ we acˡclaim you;

you are the eˡternal ˡ Father:
all creˡation ˡ worships ˡ you.

To you all angels * all the ˡ powers of ˡ heaven:
cherubim and seraphim ˡ sing in ˡ endless ˡ praise,

Holy, holy, holy, Lord * God of ˡ power and ˡ might:
heaven and ˡ earth are ˡ full of · your ˡ glory.

The glorious company of apˡostles ˡ praise you:
the noble fellowship of prophets praise you *
the white-robed ˡ army · of ˡ martyrs ˡ praise you.

Throughout the world the holy ˡ church acˡclaims you:
Father of ˡ majesˡty unˡbounded;

†   your true and only Son * worthy of ˡ all ˡ worship:
and the Holy ˡ Spirit ˡ advocate · and ˡ guide.

You Christ are the ˡ King of ˡ glory:
the eˡternal ˡ Son · of the ˡ Father.

When you became man to ˡ set us ˡ free;
you did not abˡhor the ˡ virgin's ˡ womb.

You overcame the ˈ sting of ˈ death:
and opened the kingdom of ˈ heaven · to ˈ all beˈlievers.

You are seated at God's right ˈ hand in ˈ glory:
we believe that you will ˈ come and ˈ be our ˈ judge.

Come then, Lord, and ˈ help your ˈ people:
bought with the ˈ price of ˈ your own ˈ blood:

and bring us ˈ with your ˈ saints:
to ˈ glory ˈ everˈlasting.

† Save your people Lord and ˈ bless · your inˈheritance:
govern and upˈhold them ˈ now and ˈ always.

Day by ˈ day we ˈ bless you:
we ˈ praise your ˈ name for ˈ ever.

Keep us today Lord from ˈ all ˈ sin:
have mercy ˈ on us, ˈ Lord have ˈ mercy.

Lord, show us your ˈ love and ˈ mercy:
for we ˈ put our ˈ trust in ˈ you.

In you Lord ˈ is our ˈ hope:
let us not be conˈfounded ˈ at the ˈ last.

12   GLORIA IN EXCELSIS

Glory to ˈ God · in the ˈ highest
and peace on ˈ earth am·ong ˈ men he ˈ favours.

We praise you, ◡bless you, ◡worship and ˈ glori·fy ˈ you,
we give you thanks beˈcause of ˈ your great ˈ glory,

Lord God, ' King in ' heaven,
God the ' Fa'ther Al'mighty.

Lord Jesus Christ, ⌣only ' Son · of the ' Father,
Lord ' God, ' Lamb of ' God,

you take away the ' sin · of the ' world:
have ' mer'cy up'on us.

You take away the ' sin · of the ' world:
re'ceive ' our ' prayer.

You sit at the ' Father's · right ' hand:
have ' mer'cy up'on us.

For you a'lone · are the ' Holy One;
you a'lone ' are the ' Lord;

you alone, O ' Jesus ' Christ,
together ' with the ' Holy ' Spirit,

in the glory of ' God the ' Father,
are the ' Most ' High. A'men.

13   SAVIOUR OF THE WORLD

Jesus saviour of the world * come to us ' in your ' mercy:
we look to ' you to ' save and ' help us.

By your cross and your life laid down you set your '
    people ' free:
we look to ' you to ' save and ' help us.

When they were ready to perish you ' saved · your
    dis'ciples:
we look to ' you to ' come to · our ' help.

In the greatness of your mercy loose us ˌ from our ˌ
    chains:
forgive the ˌ sins of ˌ all your ˌ people.

Make yourself known as our saviour and ˌ mighty ·
    deˌliverer:
save and ˌ help us · that ˌ we may ˌ praise you.

Come now and dwell with us ˌ Lord Christ ˌ Jesus:
hear our ˌ prayer · and be ˌ with us ˌ always.

And when you ˌ come in · your ˌ glory:
make us to be one with you * and to ˌ share the ˌ life of ·
    your ˌ kingdom.

14   HAIL, GLADDENING LIGHT

Hail, gladdening Light, of his pure glory poured
who is the immortal Father, heavenly, blest,
holiest of holies, Jesus Christ, our Lord.

Now we are come to the sun's hour of rest,
the lights of evening round us shine,
we hymn the Father, Son, and Holy Spirit divine.

Worthiest art thou at all times to be sung with
    undefiled tongue,
Son of our God, giver of life, alone!
Therefore in all the world thy glories, Lord, they own.

CANTICLES

15   THE SONG OF CHRIST'S GLORY

Christ Jesus was in the ' form of ' God:
but he did not ' cling · to e'quality · with ' God.

He emptied himself *, taking the ' form ' of a ' servant
and was ' born · in the ' likeness · of ' men.

Being found in human form he ' humbled · him'self:
and became obedient unto death, ' even ' death · on
   a ' cross.

Therefore God has ' highly · ex'alted him:
and bestowed on him the ' name a·bove ' every ' name,

that at the name of Jesus every ' knee should ' bow:
in heaven and on ' earth and ' under · the ' earth;

and every tongue confess that Jesus ' Christ is ' Lord:
to the ' glory · of ' God the ' Father.

16   THE GLORIA

Glory to the Father and ' to the ' Son:
and ' to the ' Holy ' Spirit;
as it was in the be'ginning · is ' now:
and shall be for ' ever. ' A'men.

38

Prayers and Thanksgivings

1   **The Monarch**

O Lord our heavenly Father, high and mighty, King of
kings, Lord of lords, the only ruler of princes, you look
down from your throne on all who dwell on earth: we
ask you most earnestly to look favourably on our
sovereign *lady, Queen Elizabeth.* Fill *her* with your
Holy Spirit so that *she* may love your law and walk
in your way. Give *her* health and strength; and grant
that after this life *she* may enjoy everlasting happiness
in your eternal kingdom; through Jesus Christ our
Lord. **Amen.**

Almighty God, your kingdom is eternal and your
power infinite: have mercy on the whole church. Rule
the heart of your servant *Elizabeth,* our *Queen,* so that
she, knowing whose minister *she* is, may above all
things seek your honour and glory. And grant that we
and all *her* subjects may faithfully serve, honour, and
obey *her* according to your word and ordinance;
through Jesus Christ our Lord, who lives and reigns
with you and the Holy Spirit, one God, for ever and
ever. **Amen.**

Almighty and eternal God, you teach us in your word
that the hearts of rulers are under your sovereign
control, and that you incline and turn them according
to your godly wisdom: we humbly beseech you so to
govern the heart of *Elizabeth* your servant, our *Queen,*
that in all *her* thoughts, words, and works *she* may
always seek your honour and glory and strive to

preserve your people under *her* care in prosperity, peace, and godliness. Grant this, O merciful Father, for your dear Son's sake, Jesus Christ our Lord. **Amen.**

O God, in love you provide for your people by your power and rule over them: be pleased to bless your servant *Elizabeth* our *Queen* so that under *her* this nation may be wisely governed and your church be free to serve you in godly quietness. And grant that *she*, being devoted to you with *her* whole heart and persevering in good works to the end, may by your guidance come to your eternal kingdom; through Jesus Christ our Lord. **Amen.**

Almighty God, the fountain of all goodness: we humbly beseech you to bless your servant *Queen Elizabeth* and all the members of the royal family. Fill them with your Holy Spirit; enrich them with your heavenly grace; prosper them with all happiness; and bring them to your eternal kingdom; through Jesus Christ our Lord. **Amen.**

2 Those in authority

Most gracious God, we pray for the Prime Minister, members of Cabinet and Government and all elected to the Parliament and councils of this realm. Direct and prosper all their consultations to the advancement of your glory, the good of your church, and the safety, honour, and welfare of the peoples of this land; so that peace and happiness, truth and justice, faith and godliness, may be established among us for all generations; through Jesus Christ our Lord. **Amen.**

3 The nations

Lord God Almighty, we rejoice that you are the
sovereign Lord who rules over all: may the nations of
the world hear your voice and the peoples acknowledge
you. Banish the darkness of sin and unbelief. Break
down every barrier that stands in the way of the
triumph of your Word and gospel and hasten the day
when every knee shall bow and every tongue confess
that Jesus Christ is Lord. We ask this in his name, and
to his glory. **Amen.**

4 God's church and people

Almighty and eternal God, you alone work great
marvels: send down your Holy Spirit on all bishops
and pastors and the congregations they serve. And, so
that we may all truly please you, pour on us the
continual dew of your blessing. Grant this, O Lord,
for the honour of our advocate and mediator, Jesus
Christ. **Amen.**

5 The sick

O Lord, look down from heaven, and visit and relieve
those who are ill. Look upon them with mercy;
comfort them; give them a sure confidence in you;
defend them from the attacks of the evil one; and keep
them in perpetual peace and safety; through Jesus
Christ our Lord. **Amen.**

Almighty God, you are a strong tower to all who put
their trust in you: may those who suffer find you their
defence; and may they know and feel that there is no
other name under heaven given to mankind by whom
and through whom we may receive health and salvation,
except the name of Jesus Christ our Lord. **Amen.**

Almighty and eternal God, have mercy on those who are sick. In their days of weakness strengthen their faith, lead them to repentance, and teach them to live the rest of their lives in your fear and to your glory, so that at the last they may live with you in life eternal; through Jesus Christ our Lord. **Amen.**

Lord Jesus Christ, during your earthly ministry you healed the sick: look with favour on your *servants* . . . who *are* ill at this time. Give wisdom and insight to those who care for *them*; and, if it be your will, restore *them* to health, so that *they* may live to praise you for your goodness and grace; through Jesus Christ our Lord. **Amen.**

Heavenly Father, you know the cares and fears of your children: grant that your *servant N* will remember that your care for your people is never in doubt; teach *him* to cast all *his* cares on you; give *him* quietness of mind; and fill *him* with your peace which passes all understanding; through Jesus Christ our Lord. **Amen.**

Faithfulness

Remember, O Lord, what you have worked in us and not what we deserve; and as you have called us to your service, make us worthy of our calling; through Jesus Christ our Lord. **Amen.**

For all people

O God, the Creator and Preserver of all mankind: we humbly pray that it may please you to reveal your ways to all people and your saving power to all nations. In particular we pray for your church that it may be guided and governed by your Spirit in such a way that all who profess and call themselves Christians may be led into the way of truth and hold the faith in unity of spirit, in the bond of peace, and in righteousness of life. We commend to your fatherly goodness all who are in any way afflicted or distressed [especially . . .]. Be pleased, O Lord, to comfort and relieve them according to their various needs; give them patience in their sufferings, and a happy deliverance out of their afflictions; through Jesus Christ our Lord. **Amen.**

8   **The bereaved**

Grant, O Lord, the spirit of faith and courage to those who are bereaved [and we pray especially for . . .] so that they may have strength to face the future with steadfastness and patience. May they not sorrow as those who have no hope; but may they be thankful for your great goodness to them in past years; and may they look forward with joy to the glory that you have prepared for those who love you; through Jesus Christ our Lord. **Amen.**

9   **Shortness of life**

Eternal and loving Lord, teach us to remember that life is short and to seek after heavenly wisdom. Grant that, though our bodies grow weak, we may increase in spiritual strength; so that, trusting ourselves to your care and mercy, we may accept your will and at the last enter into the joy of your eternal kingdom; through Jesus Christ our Lord. **Amen.**

10   **Education**

Most merciful Father, you teach us that the fear of the Lord is the beginning of wisdom: we pray for all who learn and all who teach in the schools and colleges of this parish (*town*, *city*, *diocese*). May those who are taught grow in the grace and knowledge of the Lord,

seek your will, and be made ready to do their duty; and
may those who instruct be filled with your love so that
they may set a good example to those committed to
their care; through Jesus Christ our Lord. **Amen.**

11   **Harvest**

Lord God Almighty, we give you thanks for all the
blessings of this life; for health and strength, for the
beauty of the world, for the kindness and love of
family and friends, for opportunities of service, and
for the harvest of land and sea. Accept our praise for
these your gifts, and make us ever mindful of our
dependence on you; for your Son, Jesus Christ's
sake. **Amen.**

Almighty God, we give you thanks and praise that you
have again fulfilled your gracious promise and given us
both seedtime and harvest. Teach us to remember that
man does not live by bread alone; and lead us and all
people to feed on your Son, Jesus Christ our Lord, who
alone is the bread of life; for this we ask in his name
and to your glory. **Amen.**

Heavenly Father, in your wisdom you have seen fit at
this time to withhold from us an abundant harvest of
the fruits of the ground. Teach us never to forget that
you give much more than we deserve; make us truly
thankful for the many blessings that you have given;
increase in us the virtues of faith, hope, and love; and
enable us humbly to submit to your will; through Jesus
Christ our Lord. **Amen.**

12   **Mission**

Almighty God, you have given your Son Jesus Christ
the name that is above every name and have taught us

that there is salvation in no one else. Grant that as we and all your people rejoice in his comfort, love, and peace, we may always prove faithful by making known to the peoples of all nations the good news of forgiveness of all sin through faith in his name; for the sake of Jesus Christ our Saviour. **Amen.**

13 **Revival**

Heavenly Father, we beg you to pour out your Spirit in these days. Awaken the unconverted and revive those who love you. Grant your people a true vision of your glory, a renewed faithfulness to your Word, and a deeper consecration to your service so that through their witness your kingdom may advance and all peoples be brought to fear your holy name; through Jesus Christ our Lord. **Amen.**

Eternal and gracious God, slow to anger and of great kindness, have mercy upon your faithless and backsliding people. We confess our lack of prayer and the many imperfections of our witness and testimony. Pardon, cleanse, and restore us, we pray; and fill us with your Spirit to proclaim the gospel of Christ to the many who have not yet been convicted of their sin and converted to their Saviour; this we ask in his name and to his glory. **Amen.**

14 **Troubled conscience**

Merciful Father, you hate nothing that you have made and have compassion on all people; and you do not desire the death of sinners, but that they should turn from their sins and be saved. In your mercy forgive us our sins; and receive and comfort us who are wearied and troubled by them. Spare us, good Lord, and turn your anger away from us, who meekly acknowledge

our wretchedness and truly repent of our misdoings. Be
quick to strengthen us so that we may live for you in
this world and with you in the world to come; through
Jesus Christ our Lord. **Amen.**

15   **A prayer from the Liturgy of John Chrysostom**

Almighty God, you have given us grace at this time to
bring before you our common supplications and have
promised that when two or three are gathered together
in your name you will grant their requests. Fulfil now,
O Lord, the desires and petitions of your servants in
ways that are most suitable for us, granting us in this
world knowledge of your truth and in the world to
come life everlasting. **Amen.**

16   **A general thanksgiving**

Almighty God, Father of all mercies,
we your unworthy servants
give you most humble and hearty thanks
for all your goodness and loving kindness
to us and all mankind.
We bless you for our creation, preservation,
and all the blessings of this life;
but above all for your immeasurable love
in the redemption of the world by our Lord Jesus
       Christ,
for the means of grace, and the hope of glory.
Give us, we pray, such a sense of all your mercies
that our hearts may be sincerely thankful,
so that we may show forth your praise,
not only with our lips, but in our lives,
by giving up ourselves to your service,
and by walking before you in holiness
and righteousness all our days;
through Jesus Christ our Lord,

to whom, with you and the Holy Spirit,
be all honour and glory, for ever and ever. Amen.

17 **For all people and for the church throughout the world**

The responses in brackets may be used

Almighty and everliving God, through the apostle
Paul, you have taught us to make prayers and
supplications and to give thanks for all men. We
humbly beg that in mercy you would receive these our
prayers which we offer to your divine majesty.

[Minister Lord in your mercy
People **Hear our prayer.**]

We pray that you will save and defend all Christian
rulers and especially your servant *Elizabeth* our *Queen*,
so that under *her* we may be governed in godliness and
peace. Grant that all who exercise authority may truly
and impartially administer justice, restrain wickedness
and vice, and maintain your true religion and virtue.
[In particular we pray for . . .]

[Minister Lord in your mercy
People **Hear our prayer.**]

We ask that you would inspire continually your church
with the spirit of truth, unity, and concord and that
you would teach all who confess your holy name to
agree in the truth of your holy Word and to live in
unity and godly love. Give grace, O heavenly Father, to
all ministers of the gospel, and especially to *N* our
bishop [and . . .], that by their life and teaching they
may set forth your true life-giving Word and rightly
administer your holy sacraments. To all your people
give your heavenly grace. And may we gathered here
receive your holy Word with reverent and humble

hearts, and may we serve you in holiness and
righteousness for the rest of our days.

[Minister   Lord in your mercy

People   **Hear our prayer.**]

We most humbly beseech you, O Lord, to comfort and
strengthen all those who in this life are in trouble,
sorrow, need, sickness, or any other adversity; [and
especially we pray for . . .]. And we bless your holy
name for all your servants who have died in your faith
and fear. Give us grace to follow their good examples
so that with them we may inherit your eternal
kingdom. Grant this, O Father, for Jesus Christ's sake,
our only mediator and advocate. [**Amen.**]

[Minister   Lord in your mercy

People   **Hear our prayer.**]

The Athanasian Creed

shall be used instead of the Apostles' Creed at Morning Prayer on
Christmas Day, *the* Epiphany, St. Matthias's Day, Easter Day,
Ascension Day, Whit Sunday (Pentecost), *on the Days of* St. John
Baptist, St. James, St. Bartholomew, St. Matthew, St. Simon and
St. Jude, *and* St. Andrew, *and on* Trinity Sunday.

Whosoever wishes to be saved
before all things it is necessary that he hold the catholic faith,
which faith, if anyone does not keep it whole and unharmed,
without doubt he will perish everlastingly.
Now, the catholic faith is this,
that we worship one God in Trinity, and Trinity in Unity,
neither confusing the Persons
nor dividing the divine Being.
For there is one Person of the Father, another of the Son,
and another of the Holy Spirit,
but the Godhead of the Father, the Son, and the Holy Spirit is all one,
their glory equal, their majesty co-eternal.
Such as the Father is, such is the Son
and such is the Holy Spirit:
the Father uncreated, the Son uncreated,
and the Holy Spirit uncreated;
the Father infinite, the Son infinite,
and the Holy Spirit infinite;
the Father eternal, the Son eternal,
and the Holy Spirit eternal;
and yet they are not three Eternals
but one Eternal,
just as they are not three Uncreateds, nor three Infinites,
but one Uncreated and one Infinite.

In the same way, the Father is almighty, the Son almighty,
and the Holy Spirit almighty;
and yet they are not three Almighties
but one Almighty.
Thus the Father is God, the Son is God,
and the Holy Spirit is God;
and yet there are not three Gods
but one God.
Thus the Father is the Lord, the Son is the Lord,
and the Holy Spirit is the Lord;
and yet not three Lords
but one Lord.

Because, just as we are compelled by Christian truth
to confess each Person singly to be both God and Lord,
so are we forbidden by the catholic religion
to say, There are three Gods, or three Lords.
The Father is from none,
not made nor created nor begotten;
the Son is from the Father alone,
not made nor created, but begotten;
the Holy Spirit is from the Father and the Son,
not made nor created nor begotten, but proceeding.
So there is one Father, not three Fathers; one Son, not three Sons;
one Holy Spirit, not three Holy Spirits.
And in this Trinity there is no before or after,
no greater or less,
but all three Persons are co-eternal with each other
and co-equal.
So that in all things, as has already been said,
the Trinity in Unity, and Unity in Trinity, is to be worshipped.
He therefore who wishes to be saved
let him think thus of the Trinity.

Furthermore, it is necessary to everlasting salvation
that he should faithfully believe the incarnation of
our Lord Jesus Christ.
Now, the right faith is that we should believe and confess
that our Lord Jesus Christ, the Son of God,
is both God and man equally.
He is God from the Being of the Father, begotten before the worlds,
and he is man from the being of his mother, born in the world;
perfect God and perfect man,
having both man's rational soul and human flesh;
equal to the Father as regards his divinity
and inferior to the Father as regards his humanity;
who, although he is God and man,
yet he is not two, but one Christ;
one, however, not by conversion of the Godhead into flesh
but by the taking up of humanity into God;
utterly one, not by confusion of human and divine being
but by unity of Christ's one Person.
For just as the rational soul and flesh are one man,
so God and man are one Christ;
who suffered for our salvation,
descended to the realm of the dead,
rose again the third day from the dead,
ascended to heaven, sat down at the right hand of the Father,
from where he will come to judge the living and the dead;
at whose coming all men will rise again with their bodies
and will give an account for their own actions,
and those who have done good will go into life everlasting
and those who have done evil into everlasting fire.
This is the catholic faith
which, if anyone does not believe faithfully and firmly,
he cannot be saved.

The Litany

or general supplication

I O God the Father, Creator of heaven and earth
have mercy on us poor sinners.
O God the Son, Redeemer of the world,
have mercy on us poor sinners.
O God the Holy Spirit, who proceeds from the Father
and the Son,
have mercy on us poor sinners.
O holy, blessed, and glorious Trinity, three persons and
one God,
have mercy on us poor sinners.

Do not remember, Lord, our sins nor the sins of our
fathers; have mercy on us. Spare us, good Lord; spare
your people, whom you have redeemed with your
precious blood, and do not be angry with us for ever.
Spare us, good Lord.

II From all evil and sin; from the crafts and assaults of the
devil; from your wrath and from eternal punishment.
Good Lord, deliver us.

From all spiritual blindness; from pride, self-conceit, and
hypocrisy; from envy, hatred, and malice; and from all
uncharitable ways.
Good Lord, deliver us.

From sexual sins; from all other deadly sin; and from all
the deceits of the world, the flesh, and the devil.
Good Lord, deliver us.

From lightning and storm; from plague, disease, and famine; from war, murder, and sudden death.
Good Lord, deliver us.

From all treason and conspiracy; from all false doctrine, heresy, and schism; from hardness of heart and contempt for your word and commandments.
Good Lord, deliver us.

By the mystery of your incarnation; by your birth and circumcision; by your baptism, fasting, and temptation.
Good Lord, deliver us.

By your agony, cross, and passion; by your precious death and burial; by your glorious resurrection and ascension; and by the coming of the Holy Spirit.
Good Lord, deliver us.

In times of trouble and in times of prosperity; in the hour of death and on the day of judgement.
Good Lord, deliver us.

III Hear us, O Lord, we pray. Be pleased to lead your church in the way of truth.
Hear us, good Lord.

Strengthen your servant *Elizabeth* our *Queen* to worship you in spirit and truth, in righteousness and holiness of life.
Hear us, good Lord.

Rule *her* heart in your faith, fear, and love, and teach *her* always to seek your honour and glory.
Hear us, good Lord.

Defend and keep *her*.
Hear us, good Lord.

Bless and preserve all members of the royal family.
Hear us, good Lord.

Give wisdom and a true knowledge of your word to all
ministers of the gospel so that in their preaching and
daily life they may declare and show its truth.
Hear us, good Lord.

At the consecration of a bishop this petition is used

May it please you to bless *this* our *brother* elected to
the office of bishop; fill *him* with your grace so that *he*
may faithfully carry out the work to which *he* is called,
to the upbuilding of the church and to the honour,
praise, and glory of your name.
Hear us, good Lord.

Give grace, wisdom, and understanding to all
members of the Government and the Houses of
Parliament.
Hear us, good Lord.

Give grace to judges and magistrates so that they may
maintain truth and execute justice.
Hear us, good Lord.

IV   Bless and keep all your people.
Hear us, good Lord.

Bring all nations to reconciliation, unity, and peace.
Hear us, good Lord.

Teach us to love and fear you and diligently to keep your
commandments.
Hear us, good Lord.

To all your people give grace so that we may meekly hear
your word, receive it with joy, and bring forth the fruit
of the Spirit.
Hear us, good Lord.

Bring all who have erred and are deceived into the way
of truth.
Hear us, good Lord.

Strengthen those who are standing firm in the faith;
comfort and encourage the faint-hearted; raise up the
fallen; and finally beat down Satan under our feet.
Hear us, good Lord.

V Help and comfort the sick and those in danger, need,
and trouble.
Hear us, good Lord.

Preserve all who travel by air, land, or sea.
Hear us, good Lord.

Sustain all women in labour.
Hear us, good Lord.

Protect all young children.
Hear us, good Lord.

Have pity on all prisoners and captives.
Hear us, good Lord.

Defend and provide for the widowed, the fatherless, the motherless, the orphaned, the desolate, and the oppressed.
Hear us, good Lord.

Have mercy on all people.
Hear us, good Lord.

Forgive our enemies, persecutors, and slanderers; and turn their hearts.
Hear us, good Lord.

Give to us and preserve for us the fruits of the earth.
Hear us, good Lord.

VI Grant us true repentance; forgive our sins, negligence, and ignorance; and empower us by your Holy Spirit to amend our lives according to your holy Word.
Hear us, good Lord.

Son of God,
we ask you to hear us.

O Lamb of God, you take away the sins of the world,
grant us your peace.

Lord, have mercy upon us.
Christ, have mercy upon us.
Lord, have mercy upon us.

THE LORD'S PRAYER

either

Our Father who art in
    heaven,
hallowed be thy name,
thy kingdom come,
thy will be done,
on earth as it is in heaven.
Give us this day
our daily bread.
And forgive us our
    trespasses
as we forgive those
who trespass against us.
And lead us not into
    temptation
but deliver us from evil.
For thine is the kingdom,
the power, and the glory,
for ever and ever. Amen.

or

Our Father in heaven,
hallowed be your name,
your kingdom come,
your will be done,
on earth as it is in heaven.
Give us today
our daily bread.
Forgive us our sins
as we forgive those
who sin against us.
Lead us not into
    temptation
but deliver us from evil.
For yours is the kingdom,
the power, and the glory,
now and for ever. Amen.

VII   Lord, do not deal with us according to our sins.
        Nor reward us according to our iniquities.

O God, our merciful Father, you do not despise the
sighing of a contrite heart nor the desires of the
sorrowful: in your mercy teach us and help us to pray
whenever we are oppressed by adversity or trouble; and
graciously hear us so that by your providence the evils
brought against us by the cunning and mischief of the
devil or man may come to nothing; and may we your
servants, with all your people, give thanks and praise
to you for ever; through Jesus Christ our Lord.
O Lord, arise, help, and deliver us for your name's sake.

O God, we have heard with our ears, and our fathers have told us, the wonderful works you did in their day and in the days before them.
O Lord, arise, help, and deliver us for your honour.

Glory be to the Father, and to the Son, and to the Holy Spirit;
**as it was in the beginning, is now,
and shall be for ever. Amen.**

Lord Jesus Christ, defend us from our enemies.
Look upon us with your grace in our afflictions.
Regard the sorrows of our hearts with your pity.
In mercy, forgive the sins of your people.
Hear our prayers with your favour.
O Son of David, have mercy on us.
Be pleased, Lord Jesus, to hear us both now and always.
O Lord, hear us.

O Lord, show us your mercy,
as we put our trust in you.

Father, in your mercy look on us in our weakness; and for the glory of your name turn from us all evils, even those we have deserved. Grant that in all our troubles our whole trust and confidence may be in you; and that we may always seek to serve you in holiness and purity of life to your honour and glory; through our only mediator and advocate, Jesus Christ our Lord.
Amen.

A prayer from the Liturgy of John Chrysostom

Almighty God, you have given us grace at this time to bring before you our common supplications and have promised that when two or three are gathered together in your name you will grant their requests. Fulfil now, O Lord, the desires and petitions of your servants in ways that are most suitable for us, granting us in this world knowledge of your truth and in the world to come life everlasting. **Amen.**

The grace of our Lord Jesus Christ,
and the love of God,
and the fellowship of the Holy Spirit,
be with us all evermore. Amen.

Holy Communion
First Order

The background to Holy Communion is given in a number of
Bible passages. Exodus 12 tells the story of the Passover. Jesus
developed the Passover meal into the Lord's Supper or Holy
Communion, as described in the first three Gospels and in
1 Corinthians 11: 23–34.

We welcome to the Lord's table all baptized believers who are
communicant members of other Christian churches (see Canon
B15A). Confirmation classes are arranged for those who wish to
become communicant members of the Church of England. Please
inform the minister(s) if you are interested.

1   *The minister welcomes the people, and announces the opening*
HYMN.

2
All   **Almighty God,**
to whom all hearts are open,
all desires known,
and from whom no secrets are hidden:
cleanse the thoughts of our hearts
by the inspiration of your Holy Spirit,
so that we may perfectly love you,
and worthily magnify your holy name,
through Christ our Lord. Amen.

3   THE COMMANDMENTS

Minister   God spoke all these words saying: I am the Lord your
         God.

         You shall have no gods other than me.

         You shall not make for yourself an idol (in the form of
         anything in heaven above or on the earth beneath, or in
         the waters below. You shall not bow down to them nor
         worship them, for I, the Lord your God, am a jealous
         God who punishes the children for the sin of the fathers
         to the third and fourth generations of those who hate
         me, but I show love to thousands who love me and
         keep my commandments).

         You shall not misuse the name of the Lord your God
         (for the Lord will not hold anyone guiltless who
         misuses his name).

         Remember to keep the Sabbath day holy. (Six days you
         shall labour and do all your work, but the seventh day
         is a Sabbath to the Lord your God. On it you shall not
         do any work, neither you nor your son or daughter, nor
         your manservant or maidservant, nor your animals, nor
         the foreigner living among you. For in six days the Lord
         made the heavens and the earth, the sea and all that is
         in them, but he rested on the seventh day. Therefore
         the Lord blessed the Sabbath day and made it holy.)

All   **Lord, have mercy on us, and incline our hearts to
         keep these laws.**

Minister   Honour your father and your mother (so that you may
         live long in the land the Lord your God is giving you).

You shall not commit murder.

You shall not commit adultery.

You shall not steal.

You shall not bear false witness against your neighbour.

You shall not covet (your neighbour's house. You shall not covet your neighbour's wife, nor his manservant, his maidservant, his ox or donkey, nor anything that belongs to him).

All **Lord, have mercy on us, and write all these your laws on our hearts, we beseech you.**

4 THE COLLECTS *(special prayers)* FOR THE MONARCH *may be used (p. 39).*

5 THE COLLECT OF THE DAY *(pp. 84 ff.).*

6 THE SCRIPTURE READINGS

The first is usually from a New Testament letter or alternatively from the Old Testament and the second is always from one of the four Gospels.

It is customary to stand for the Gospel reading.

After each reading the reader says:

This is the word of the Lord.
All **Thanks be to God.**

7   THE NICENE CREED

All   I believe in one God, the Father Almighty,
Maker of heaven and earth,
and of all things, visible and invisible.

I believe in one Lord Jesus Christ,
the only begotten Son of God,
begotten of the Father before all ages,
God from God, Light from Light,
true God from true God, begotten, not made,
of one being with the Father.
Through him all things were made.
For us and for our salvation
he came down from heaven.
He became incarnate by the Holy Spirit
of the virgin Mary, and was made man.
For our sake he was crucified under Pontius Pilate.
He suffered death and was buried.
On the third day he rose again
according to the Scriptures.
He ascended into heaven
and is seated at the right hand of the Father.
He shall come again in glory
to judge the living and the dead,
and his kingdom will have no end.

I believe in the Holy Spirit,
the Lord, the giver of life,
who proceeds from the Father and the Son.
With the Father and the Son
he is worshipped and glorified.
He spoke through the prophets.

I believe one catholic, and apostolic church,
and I acknowledge one baptism for the remission of
    sins.
I look for the resurrection of the dead,
and the life of the world to come. Amen.

8   THE NOTICES *and* BANNS OF MARRIAGE *are announced after which the* OFFERING *is brought forward and received.*

9   A HYMN *may be sung.*

10   THE SERMON *is preached.*

11   THE PRAYERS *(see e.g. pp. 39 ff.).*
     Each prayer may end with **Amen**, *or this response:*

Minister   Lord, in your mercy
All   **hear our prayer.**

     The time of prayer may be ended with this response:

Minister   Merciful Father,
All   **accept these prayers for the sake of your Son,**
           our Saviour Jesus Christ. Amen.

12   A HYMN *may be sung, during which the minister prepares the bread and wine.*

13   *The minister reads this* EXHORTATION *and* INVITATION:

The Scriptures teach that those who intend to eat the
bread and drink the cup of the Lord must examine
their lives and repent of their sins. They must come to
the Lord's table with a penitent heart and firm faith.
Above all, they should come giving thanks to God for
his love towards us in Christ Jesus.

You who truly and earnestly repent of your sins and
are reconciled and at peace with your neighbours and
intend to lead a new life, following the
commandments of God and walking in his holy ways,
draw near by faith, take this holy sacrament for your
encouragement, and make your humble confession to
Almighty God.

14   CONFESSION

All   **Almighty God, Father of our Lord Jesus Christ,**
        maker of all things, judge of all men,
        we acknowledge and confess our many sins,
        which we have committed by thought, word, and
        **   deed,**
        against your divine majesty,
        provoking your wrath and indignation against us.
        We earnestly repent,
        and are truly sorry for all our misdoings.
        The memory of them grieves us.
        The burden of them is more than we can bear.
        Have mercy on us, most merciful Father.
        For your Son our Lord Jesus Christ's sake
        forgive us all that is past,
        and grant that from now on we may always

serve and please you in lives wholly renewed by your
   Spirit,
to the honour and glory of your name,
through Jesus Christ our Lord. **Amen.**

15   *The minister declares* GOD'S FORGIVENESS, *and reads one or*
         more of the following PROMISES *of assurance from the Bible:*

Almighty God our heavenly Father, who in his great
mercy has promised forgiveness of sins to all who turn to
him with heartfelt repentance and true faith: be merciful
to you, pardon and deliver you from all your sins,
confirm and strengthen you in all goodness, and bring
you to eternal life, through Jesus Christ our Lord. **Amen.**

Listen to our Lord Jesus Christ's words of assurance to
all who truly turn to him:

Come to me, all you who are weary and burdened, and
I will give you rest. *Matthew 11: 28*

For God so loved the world that he gave his one and
only Son that whoever believes in him shall not perish
but have eternal life. *John 3: 16*

The apostle Paul says:
Here is a trustworthy saying that deserves full
acceptance: Christ Jesus came into the world to save
sinners. *1 Timothy 1: 15*

The apostle John also says:
If anybody does sin, we have one who speaks to the
Father in our defence—Jesus Christ, the Righteous One.
He is the atoning sacrifice for our sins. *1 John 2: 1–2*

16

Minister	Lift up your hearts.
People	**We lift them up to the Lord.**

Minister	Let us give thanks to the Lord our God.
People	**It is right to give him thanks and praise.**

Minister   It is indeed right, our duty and joy, that we should always and everywhere give thanks to you, O Lord, holy Father, mighty Creator, and eternal God.

A seasonal PREFACE *may be included here (see pp. 71 f.).*

All   **Therefore with angels and archangels,**
and with the whole company of heaven,
we praise and magnify your glorious name,
evermore praising you, and saying:

Holy, holy, holy, Lord God of hosts,
heaven and earth are full of your glory.
Glory be to you, O Lord most high. Amen.

17

All   **We do not presume to come to this your table,**
merciful Lord, trusting in our own righteousness,
but in your abundant and great mercies.
We are not even worthy
to gather up the crumbs under your table.
But you are the same Lord,
who delights in showing mercy.
Grant us, therefore, gracious Lord,
so to eat this bread and drink this wine
that our bodies and souls
may be cleansed by Christ's body and blood

**and that we may evermore dwell in him,
and he in us. Amen.**

18 *The minister says this* PRAYER OF CONSECRATION:

Almighty God, our heavenly Father, in your tender
mercy you gave your only Son Jesus Christ to suffer
death upon the cross for our redemption. He made
there, by his once and for all offering of himself, a full,
perfect, and sufficient sacrifice for the sins of the whole
world. He instituted and in his holy gospel commands
us to continue a perpetual memory of his precious
death until he comes again.

Hear us, O merciful Father, we humbly pray, and
grant that we who receive this bread and wine
according to your Son Jesus Christ's holy institution,
in remembrance of his death and passion, may be
partakers of his most blessed body and blood.

On the night that he was betrayed he took bread (*the
minister takes the bread*) and, when he had given thanks,
he broke it (*he breaks the bread*) and gave it to his
disciples, saying: Take, eat; this is my body which is
given for you. Do this in remembrance of me.

In the same way, after supper, he took the cup (*he
takes the cup*) and, when he had given thanks, he gave
it to them, saying: Drink this, all of you; this is my
blood of the new covenant which is shed for you and
for many for the forgiveness of sins. Do this, as often as
you drink it, in remembrance of me. **Amen.**

19   THE ADMINISTRATION

These words are said at the administration of the bread:

May the body of our Lord Jesus Christ, which was
given for you, preserve your body and soul to eternal
life. Take and eat this in remembrance that Christ died
for you and feed on him in your heart by faith with
thanksgiving.

These words are said at the administration of the cup:

May the blood of our Lord Jesus Christ, which was
shed for you, preserve your body and soul to eternal
life. Drink this in remembrance that Christ's blood was
shed for you and be thankful.

20   THE LORD'S PRAYER:

either	*or*
All Our Father who art in heaven,	Our Father in heaven,
hallowed be thy name,	hallowed be your name,
thy kingdom come,	your kingdom come,
thy will be done,	your will be done,
on earth as it is in heaven.	on earth as it is in heaven.
Give us this day	Give us today
our daily bread.	our daily bread.
And forgive us our trespasses	Forgive us our sins
as we forgive those	as we forgive those
who trespass against us.	who sin against us.
And lead us not into temptation	Lead us not into temptation
	but deliver us from evil.
	For yours is the kingdom,

but deliver us from evil.
For thine is the kingdom,
the power, and the glory,
for ever and ever. Amen.

the power, and the glory,
now and for ever. Amen.

21   PRAYER:

either

All   Almighty God,
we thank you for feeding us with the spiritual food
of the body and blood of your Son Jesus Christ.
Through him we offer you our souls and bodies
to be a living sacrifice.
Send us out into the world
in the power of your Spirit,
to live and work
to your praise and glory. Amen.

or

Almighty and everliving God,
we thank you for reassuring us at this communion
of your favour and goodness towards us;
that we are truly members of the body of your Son;
and that we are also heirs, through hope,
of your eternal kingdom.
We humbly beg you, heavenly Father,
to keep us as faithful members of your church
and to strengthen us by your Spirit
so that we may fulfil those good works
which you have prepared for us to do;
through Jesus Christ our Lord. Amen.

22 *GLORIA IN EXCELSIS (p. 35) may be used or a* HYMN *may be sung. The minister may say* THE BLESSING *(p. 24)*

Go in peace and serve the Lord.
All **In the name of Christ. Amen.**

SEASONAL PREFACES

Christmas Day

because you gave your only Son Jesus Christ to be born for us. By the work of the Holy Spirit he was made man, born of the virgin Mary his mother; but without sin, to make us clean from all sin. Therefore . . .

Easter Day

but we must above all praise you for the glorious resurrection of your Son Jesus Christ our Lord. He is the Passover lamb who was offered for us and has taken away the sin of the world. By his death he has destroyed death; and by his rising to life again he has restored eternal life to us. Therefore . . .

Ascension Day

through your most dearly loved Son Jesus Christ our Lord, who after his most glorious resurrection appeared to the apostles and in their sight ascended into heaven to prepare a place for us so that where he is, there we might also ascend and reign with him in glory. Therefore . . .

Whit-Sunday (Pentecost)

through Jesus Christ our Lord, according to whose promise the Holy Spirit came down from heaven upon the apostles to teach them and to lead them into all truth. He gave them boldness and zeal to preach the gospel to all nations, by which we have been brought out of darkness and error into the true knowledge of you and of your Son Jesus Christ. Therefore . . .

Trinity Sunday

for you are one God, one Lord; not one person but three persons in one substance. For what we believe of the glory of the Father we also believe of the Son and of the Holy Spirit, without any difference or inequality. Therefore . . .

Holy Communion

Second Order

*The background to Holy Communion is given in a number of
Bible passages. Exodus 12 tells the story of the Passover. Jesus
developed the Passover meal into the Lord's Supper or Holy
Communion, as described in the first three Gospels and in
1 Corinthians 11: 23–34.*

*We welcome to the Lord's table all baptized believers who are
communicant members of other Christian churches (see Canon
B15A). Confirmation classes are arranged for those who wish to
become communicant members of the Church of England. Please
inform the minister(s) if you are interested.*

1   *The minister welcomes the people saying:*

Christ is our peace.
He has reconciled us to God in one body by the cross.
We meet in his name and share his peace.

either

The Lord be with you

All   **and with your spirit.**

or

The peace of the Lord be always with you

All   **and with you.**

A sign of peace may be exchanged.

2   A HYMN *may be sung.*

3

All   **Almighty God,**
to whom all hearts are open,
all desires known,
and from whom no secrets are hidden:
cleanse the thoughts of our hearts
by the inspiration of your Holy Spirit,
so that we may perfectly love you,
and worthily magnify your holy name,
through Christ our Lord. Amen.

4   THE COLLECT *(special prayer)* OF THE DAY *(pp. 84 ff.).*

5   THE PRAYERS, *including remembrance of the monarch and those in authority (see e.g. pp. 39 ff.).*
Each prayer may end with **Amen,** *or this response:*

Minister   Lord, in your mercy
All   **hear our prayer.**

The time of prayer may be ended with this response:

Minister   Merciful Father,
All   **accept these prayers for the sake of your Son,**
our Saviour Jesus Christ. Amen.

6   *GLORIA IN EXCELSIS (p. 35) may be used or another* HYMN *may be sung.*

7   THE SCRIPTURE READINGS

The first is usually from a New Testament letter or alternatively from the Old Testament and the second is always from one of the four Gospels.

It is customary to stand for the Gospel reading.

After each reading the reader says:

This is the word of the Lord.

All   **Thanks be to God.**

8   THE NICENE CREED

All   **I believe in one God, the Father Almighty,
Maker of heaven and earth,
and of all things, visible and invisible.**

**I believe in one Lord Jesus Christ,
the only begotten Son of God,
begotten of the Father before all ages,
God from God, Light from Light,
true God from true God, begotten, not made,
of one being with the Father.
Through him all things were made.
For us and for our salvation
he came down from heaven.
He became incarnate by the Holy Spirit
of the virgin Mary, and was made man.
For our sake he was crucified under Pontius Pilate.
He suffered death and was buried.
On the third day he rose again
according to the Scriptures.
He ascended into heaven**

and is seated at the right hand of the Father.
He shall come again in glory
to judge the living and the dead,
and his kingdom will have no end.

I believe in the Holy Spirit,
the Lord, the giver of life,
who proceeds from the Father and the Son.
With the Father and the Son
he is worshipped and glorified.
He spoke through the prophets.
I believe one catholic, and apostolic church,
and I acknowledge one baptism for the remission of
    sins.
I look for the resurrection of the dead,
and the life of the world to come. Amen.

9   THE NOTICES *and* BANNS OF MARRIAGE *are announced, after
which the* OFFERING *is received.*

10   A HYMN *may be sung.*

11   THE SERMON *is preached.*

12   A HYMN *may be sung, during which the minister prepares the
bread and wine.*

13   THE COMMANDMENTS *(p. 61) or this* SUMMARY OF THE LAW
is said:

Minister   Our Lord Jesus Christ said:
           The most important commandment is this: Hear O
           Israel, the Lord our God, the Lord is One. Love the

Lord your God with all your heart and with all your soul and with all your mind and with all your strength. The second is this: Love your neighbour as yourself. There is no commandment greater than these. *Mark 12: 29–31*

All   **Lord, have mercy on us,
and incline our hearts to keep these laws.**

14   *The minister reads these* SENTENCES OF SCRIPTURE:

Listen to our Lord Jesus Christ's words of assurance to all who truly turn to him:

Come to me, all you who are weary and burdened, and I will give you rest. *Matthew 11: 28*

For God so loved the world that he gave his one and only Son that whoever believes in him shall not perish but have eternal life. *John 3: 16*

The apostle Paul says:
Here is a trustworthy saying that deserves full acceptance: Christ Jesus came into the world to save sinners. *1 Timothy 1: 15*

The apostle John says:
If anybody does sin, we have one who speaks to the Father in our defence—Jesus Christ, the Righteous One. He is the atoning sacrifice for our sins. *1 John 2: 1–2*

The apostle Paul also says:
Whenever you eat this bread and drink this cup, you proclaim the Lord's death until he comes. Therefore whoever eats the bread and drinks the cup in an

unworthy manner will be guilty of sinning against the body and blood of the Lord. A man ought to examine himself before he eats of the bread and drinks of the cup. *1 Corinthians 11: 26–28*

15 CONFESSION

All **Most merciful Father, our Creator and Judge,**
we acknowledge and confess
that we have sinned against you
by thought, word, and deed.
We have not loved you with all our heart;
and we have not loved our neighbours as ourselves.
We earnestly repent, and are truly sorry for all our
sins.
For your Son our Lord Jesus Christ's sake forgive us.
And strengthen us to serve and obey you
in lives wholly renewed by your Spirit;
through Jesus Christ our Lord. Amen.

16 *The minister declares* GOD'S FORGIVENESS:

Almighty God our heavenly Father, who has promised forgiveness to all who repent and have true faith in him, be merciful to you, pardon and set you free from all your sins, strengthen you in his service, and bring you to eternal life; through Jesus Christ our Lord. **Amen.**

17
All **We do not presume to come to this your table,**
merciful Lord, trusting in our own righteousness,
but in your abundant and great mercies.

We are not even worthy
to gather up the crumbs under your table.
But you are the same Lord,
who delights in showing mercy.
Grant us, therefore, gracious Lord,
so to eat this bread and drink this wine
that we may feed on Christ in our hearts
by faith with thanksgiving;
through Jesus Christ our Lord. Amen.

18

Minister   Lift up your hearts.
People   **We lift them up to the Lord.**

Minister   Let us give thanks to the Lord our God.
People   **It is right to give him thanks and praise.**

Minister   It is indeed right, our duty and joy, always and everywhere, to give you thanks and praise, holy Father, heavenly King, Almighty and eternal God, through Jesus Christ your only Son our Lord.

We especially praise you because in your tender mercy you sent him to suffer death upon the cross for our redemption. There he made, by his once and for all offering of himself, a full, perfect, and sufficient sacrifice for the sins of the whole world. Through him you have freed us from the slavery of sin.

People   **Therefore with angels and archangels,
and with the whole company of heaven,
we praise and magnify your glorious name,
evermore praising you, and saying:**

Holy, holy, holy,
Lord God of power and might,
heaven and earth are full of your glory.
Hosanna in the highest.

Minister Hear us, merciful Father, we humbly pray, and grant
that we who eat this bread and drink this wine
according to your Son Jesus Christ's holy institution,
in remembrance of his death and passion, may be
partakers of his most blessed body and blood.

For on the night that he was betrayed he took bread
(*the minister takes the bread*) and, when he had given
thanks, he broke it (*he breaks the bread*) and said, This is
my body, which is given for you; do this in
remembrance of me.

In the same way, after supper, he took the cup (*he takes*
the cup) saying, This cup is the new covenant in my
blood; do this, whenever you drink it, in remembrance
of me. **Amen.**

19   THE ADMINISTRATION

These words are said at the administration of the bread:

either

May the body of our Lord Jesus Christ, which was
given for you, preserve your body and soul to eternal
life. Take and eat this in remembrance that Christ died
for you and feed on him in your heart by faith with
thanksgiving.

or

Take and eat this in remembrance that Christ died for you and be thankful.

These words are said at the administration of the cup:

either

May the blood of our Lord Jesus Christ, which was shed for you, preserve your body and soul to eternal life. Drink this in remembrance that Christ's blood was shed for you and be thankful.

or

Drink this in remembrance that Christ's blood was shed for you and be thankful.

20   THE LORD'S PRAYER:

either	*or*
Our Father who art in heaven, **hallowed be thy name,** **thy kingdom come,** **thy will be done,** **on earth as it is in heaven.** **Give us this day** **our daily bread.** **And forgive us our trespasses** **as we forgive those** **who trespass against us.** **And lead us not into temptation**	**Our Father in heaven,** **hallowed be your name,** **your kingdom come,** **your will be done,** **on earth as it is in heaven.** **Give us today** **our daily bread.** **Forgive us our sins** **as we forgive those** **who sin against us.** **Lead us not into temptation** **but deliver us from evil.** **For yours is the kingdom,**

All

but deliver us from evil.
For thine is the kingdom,
the power, and the glory,
for ever and ever. Amen.

the power, and the glory,
now and for ever. Amen.

21   PRAYER:

either

All   Almighty God,
we thank you for feeding us with the spiritual food
of the body and blood of your Son Jesus Christ.
Through him we offer you our souls and bodies
to be a living sacrifice.
Send us out into the world
in the power of your Spirit,
to live and work
to your praise and glory. Amen.

or

Almighty and everliving God,
we thank you for reassuring us at this communion
of your favour and goodness towards us;
that we are truly members of the body of your Son;
and that we are also heirs, through hope,
of your eternal kingdom.
We humbly beg you, heavenly Father,
to keep us as faithful members of your church
and to strengthen us by your Spirit
so that we may fulfil those good works
which you have prepared for us to do;
through Jesus Christ our Lord. Amen.

22   ACCLAMATION

All   **Christ has died:**
         Christ is risen
         Christ will come again.

23   *GLORIA IN EXCELSIS (p. 35) may be used* or a HYMN *may be sung.*
         The minister may say THE BLESSING *(p. 24)*

         Go in peace and serve the Lord.
All   **In the name of Christ. Amen.**

The Collects

with Epistle and Gospel readings

SUNDAYS AND MAJOR FESTIVALS

Advent Sunday

Year 1   Romans 13: 8–14   Matthew 21: 1–13
Year 2   1 Corinthians 1: 3–9   Mark 13: 33–37

Almighty God, give us grace to cast away the works of darkness and to put on the armour of light, now in the time of this mortal life, in which your Son Jesus Christ came to us in great humility so that on the last day, when he will come again in his glorious majesty to judge the living and the dead, we may rise to the life immortal, through him who lives and reigns with you and the Holy Spirit, one God, now and for ever. **Amen.**

(This collect is to be said daily during Advent until Christmas Eve)

Advent 2

Year 1   Romans 15: 4–13   Luke 21: 25–33
Year 2   2 Peter 3: 8–14   Mark 1: 1–8

Blessed Lord, who caused the holy Scriptures to be written for our learning, grant that we may so hear, read, mark, learn, and inwardly digest them that through patience and the comfort of your holy Word, we may embrace and for ever hold fast the joyful hope of everlasting life, which you have given us in our Saviour Jesus Christ. **Amen.**

Advent 3

| Year 1 | 1 Corinthians 4: 1–5 | Matthew 11: 2–10 |
| Year 2 | 1 Thessalonians 5: 16–24 | John 1: 6–8, 19–28 |

Lord Jesus Christ, who at your first coming sent your messenger John the Baptist to prepare the way for you, grant that the ministers and stewards of your truth may so make ready your way, by turning the hearts of the disobedient to the wisdom of the just, that at your second coming to judge the world, we may be found an acceptable people in your sight; for you live and reign with the Father and the Holy Spirit, one God, now and for ever. **Amen.**

Advent 4

| Year 1 | Philippians 4: 4–7 | John 1: 19–28 |
| Year 2 | Romans 16: 25–27 | Luke 1: 26–38 |

Lord, come among us, we pray, with your power and help us with your great might so that, although we are hindered by our sins and wickedness from running the race set before us, your bountiful grace and mercy may speedily help and deliver us through the work of your Son our Lord to whom with you and the Holy Spirit be honour and glory now and for ever. **Amen.**

Christmas Day (*The Birthday of Christ*)

| Year 1 | Hebrews 1: 1–12 | John 1: 1–18 |
| Year 2 | Titus 2: 11–14 | Luke 2: 1–14 |

Almighty God, who gave us your only Son to take our nature upon him and to be born of a pure virgin, grant that we, who are born again in him and made your children by adoption and grace, may daily be renewed by your Holy Spirit through our Lord Jesus Christ, who lives and reigns with you and the Spirit, one God, now and for ever. **Amen.**

Sunday after Christmas

Year 1	Galatians 4: 1–7	Matthew 1: 18–25
Year 2	Colossians 3: 12–21	Luke 2: 22–40

Almighty God, who gave us your only Son to take our nature upon him and to be born of a pure virgin, grant that we, who are born again in him and made your children by adoption and grace, may daily be renewed by your Holy Spirit through our Lord Jesus Christ, who lives and reigns with you and the Spirit, one God, now and for ever. **Amen.**

The Circumcision of Christ (1 January)

Year 1	Romans 4: 8–15	Luke 2: 15–21
Year 2	Galatians 4: 4–7	Luke 2: 15–21

Almighty God, who caused your blessed Son to be circumcised and obedient to the law for mankind, grant us the true circumcision of the Spirit so that, our hearts and bodies being dead to all sinful desires, we may obey your holy will in all things through your Son Jesus Christ our Lord. **Amen.**

(This collect is to be used until 5 January)

The Epiphany (6 January)

Year 1	Ephesians 3: 1–13	Matthew 2: 1–12
Year 2	Isaiah 49: 1–6	Matthew 2: 1–12

O God, who revealed your only Son to the Gentiles by the leading of a star, mercifully grant that we, who know you now by faith, may after this life enjoy the splendour of your glorious Godhead, through Jesus Christ our Lord. **Amen.**

Epiphany 1

Year 1	Romans 12: 1–5	Luke 2: 41–52
Year 2	Acts 10: 34–38	Mark 1: 7–11

Merciful Lord, receive the prayers of your people who call upon you and grant that we may know those things we ought to do and also have the grace and power faithfully to perform them, through Jesus Christ our Lord. **Amen.**

Epiphany 2

Year 1	Romans 12: 6–16	John 2: 1–11
Year 2	1 Corinthians 6: 12–20	John 1: 35–42

Almighty and everlasting God, ruler of all things in heaven and on earth: in mercy hear the prayers of your people and grant us your peace throughout our lives; through Jesus Christ our Lord. **Amen.**

Epiphany 3

Year 1	Romans 12: 17–21	Matthew 8: 1–13
Year 2	Hebrews 4: 14–16	Mark 10: 33–45

Almighty and everlasting God, in mercy look upon our weakness and in all our dangers and necessities stretch out your right hand to help and defend us, through Jesus Christ our Lord. **Amen.**

Epiphany 4

Year 1	Romans 13: 1–7	Matthew 8: 23–34
Year 2	Ephesians 5: 21–33	John 6: 60–69

Lord God, you know that we are in the midst of such dangers and that we cannot always stand upright because of the frailty of our nature: grant us strength and protection to support us in all dangers and carry us through all temptations, through Jesus Christ our Lord. **Amen.**

Epiphany 5

Year 1	Colossians 3: 12–17	Matthew 13: 24–30
Year 2	2 Corinthians 8: 7–15	Mark 5: 21–43

Heavenly Father, keep your household the church continually in your true religion so that we may lean only on the hope of your heavenly grace and always be defended by your mighty power, through Jesus Christ our Lord. **Amen.**

Epiphany 6

Year 1	1 John 3: 1–8	Matthew 24: 23–31
Year 2	Galatians 5: 13–18	Luke 9: 51–62

O God, whose blessed Son was revealed so that he might destroy the works of the devil and make us children of God and heirs of eternal life, grant that we, who have this hope, may purify ourselves as he is pure so that, when he shall appear in power and great glory, we may be made like him in his eternal and glorious kingdom, where he lives and reigns with you, the Father, and with you, the Holy Spirit, one God, now and for ever. **Amen.**

Septuagesima (*Third Sunday before Lent*)

Year 1	1 Corinthians 9: 24–27	Matthew 20: 1–16
Year 2	Hebrews 2: 9–11	Mark 10: 2–16

Lord, hear with favour the prayers of your people so that we, who deserve to be punished for our offences, may mercifully be delivered by your goodness, for the glory of your name, through Jesus Christ our Saviour, who is alive and reigns with you and the Holy Spirit, one God, now and for ever. **Amen.**

Sexagesima (*Second Sunday before Lent*)

Year 1	2 Corinthians 11: 16–31	Luke 8: 4–15
Year 2	Ephesians 4: 30–5: 2	John 6: 41–51

Lord God, you know that we do not put our trust in anything that we do: mercifully defend us by your power against all adversity, through Jesus Christ our Lord. **Amen.**

Quinquagesima (*Sunday before Lent*)

Year 1	1 Corinthians 13: 1–13	Luke 18: 31–43
Year 2	1 Corinthians 7: 32–35	Mark 1: 21–28

Lord, you have taught us that whatever we do without
love is worth nothing: send your Holy Spirit and pour
into our hearts that most excellent gift of love, the true
bond of peace and all virtues; for without love whoever
lives is reckoned dead by you. Grant this for the sake of
your only Son, Jesus Christ our Lord. **Amen.**

Ash Wednesday (*First day of Lent*)

Year 1	Joel 2: 12–17	Matthew 6: 16–21
Year 2	2 Corinthians 5: 16–6: 2	Matthew 6: 1–6, 16–18

Almighty and everlasting God, you hate nothing that
you have made and forgive the sins of all who are
penitent: make in us new and contrite hearts so that,
lamenting our sins and acknowledging our
wretchedness, we may receive from you, the God of all
mercy, perfect remission and forgiveness through Jesus
Christ our Lord. **Amen.**

(This collect is to be said daily during Lent)

Lent 1

Year 1	2 Corinthians 6: 1–10	Matthew 4: 1–11
Year 2	1 Peter 3: 18–22	Mark 1: 12–15

Lord Jesus Christ, who for our sake fasted forty days
and forty nights, give us grace so to discipline ourselves
that we may always obey your will in righteousness
and true holiness to the honour and glory of your
name; for you live and reign with the Father and Holy
Spirit, one God, now and for ever. **Amen.**

Lent 2

Year 1	1 Thessalonians 4: 1–8	Matthew 15: 21–28
Year 2	Romans 8: 31*b*–34	Mark 9: 2–10

Almighty God, you see that we have no power of our own to help ourselves: keep us both outwardly in our bodies and inwardly in our souls so that we may be defended from all ills that may befall the body and from all evil thoughts that may assault and hurt the soul, through Jesus Christ our Lord. **Amen.**

Lent 3

Year 1	Ephesians 5: 1–14	Luke 11: 14–28
Year 2	1 Corinthians 1: 22–25	John 2: 13–25

Almighty God, consider the heartfelt desires of your servants and stretch out the right hand of your majesty to defend us against all our enemies, through Jesus Christ our Lord. **Amen.**

Lent 4

Year 1	Galatians 4: 21–31	John 6: 1–15
Year 2	Ephesians 2: 4–10	John 3: 14–21

Grant, Almighty God, that we, who deserve to be punished for our evil deeds, may by your grace and mercy be spared through Jesus Christ our Lord. **Amen.**

Lent 5

Year 1	Hebrews 9: 11–15	John 8: 46–59
Year 2	Hebrews 5: 7–9	John 12: 20–33

Almighty God, look mercifully upon your people so that by your great goodness we may be always governed and preserved both in body and soul, through Jesus Christ our Lord. **Amen.**

Sunday before Easter

Year 1	Philippians 2: 5–11	Matthew 27: 1–54
Year 2	Philippians 2: 5–11	Mark 15: 1–39

Almighty and everlasting God, who in your tender love towards mankind sent your Son our Saviour Jesus Christ to take upon him our nature and to suffer death upon the cross so that all mankind should follow the example of his great humility, grant that we may both follow the example of his patience and also have our part in his resurrection, through Jesus Christ our Lord. **Amen.**

(This collect is used daily until Maundy Thursday)

Monday before Easter

Year 1	Isaiah 63: 1–19	Mark 14: 1–72
Year 2	Isaiah 42: 1–7	John 12: 1–11

Tuesday before Easter

Year 1	Isaiah 50: 5–11	Mark 15: 1–39
Year 2	Isaiah 49: 1–6	John 13: 21–38

Wednesday before Easter

Year 1	Hebrews 9: 16–28	Luke 22: 1–71
Year 2	Isaiah 50: 4–9*a*	Matthew 26: 14–25

Thursday before Easter (*Maundy Thursday*)

Year 1	1 Corinthians 11: 17–34	Luke 23: 1–49
Year 2	1 Corinthians 11: 23–26	John 13: 1–15

The Good Friday Collects

Year 1	Hebrews 10: 1–25	John 19: 1–37
Year 2	Hebrews 4: 14–5: 10	John 18: 1–19, 42

Almighty God, in mercy look on this your family, for which our Lord Jesus Christ was willing to be betrayed and given up into the hands of wicked men and to suffer death upon the cross, who now lives and reigns with you and the Holy Spirit, one God, for ever and ever. **Amen.**

Almighty and everlasting God, by whose Spirit the whole body of the church is governed and sanctified, receive our prayers which we offer to you for the many different members of your holy church so that every one in his vocation and ministry may truly and devoutly serve you through Jesus Christ our Lord. **Amen.**

Merciful God, you have made all people and hate nothing that you have made, nor do you desire the death of sinners but rather that they should be converted and live: have mercy on the Jewish people and all who do not know you or who deny the faith of Christ crucified. Take from them all ignorance, hardness of heart, and contempt for your Word and bring them home to your fold, blessed Lord, so that we may all become one flock under one shepherd, Jesus Christ our Lord, who lives and reigns with you and the Holy Spirit, one God, for ever and ever. **Amen.**

Easter Eve

Years
1 and 2

1 Peter 3: 17–22   Matthew 27: 57–66

Lord, into the death of whose dear Son our Saviour
Jesus Christ we have been baptized, grant that we may
continually put to death our sinful desires and be
buried with him so that we may pass through the grave
and gate of death to our joyful resurrection through
the merits of him who died, was buried, and rose again
for us, your Son Jesus Christ our Lord. **Amen.**

Easter Day

Year 1
Year 2

Colossians 3: 1–7   John 20: 1–10
Romans 6: 1–11   Mark 16: 1–8

Almighty God, through your only Son Jesus Christ you
have conquered death and opened to us the gate of
everlasting life: by your grace put good desires into our
minds and, in your mercy, help us to bring them to
their fulfilment, through Jesus Christ our Lord, who
lives and reigns with you and the Holy Spirit, one God,
for ever and ever. **Amen.**

Monday in Easter week

Years
1 and 2

Acts 10: 34–43   Luke 24: 13–35

Tuesday in Easter week

Years
1 and 2

Acts 13: 26–41   Luke 24: 36–48

94

Easter 1

| Year 1 | 1 John 5: 4–12 | John 20: 19–23 |
| Year 2 | 1 John 5: 1–6 | John 20: 19–31 |

Almighty Father, who gave your only Son to die for our
sins and to rise again for our justification, grant that
we may put away the old leaven of malice and
wickedness and always serve you in purity and truth
through Jesus Christ our Lord. **Amen.**

Easter 2

| Year 1 | 1 Peter 2: 19–25 | John 10: 11–16 |
| Year 2 | 1 John 2: 1–6 | Luke 24: 35–48 |

Almighty God, who gave your only Son for us to be
both a sacrifice for sin and an example of godly life,
give us grace so that we may always receive with
thankfulness the immeasurable benefit of his sacrifice,
and try day by day to follow in the steps of his most
holy life, through Jesus Christ our Lord. **Amen.**

Easter 3

| Year 1 | 1 Peter 2: 11–17 | John 16: 16–22 |
| Year 2 | 1 John 3: 1–2 | John 10: 11–18 |

Almighty God, you show the light of your truth to
those who are in error so that they may return into the
way of righteousness: grant to all who are admitted
into the fellowship of Christ's religion that they may
reject everything that is contrary to their profession
and follow whatever is in agreement with it, through
Jesus Christ our Lord. **Amen.**

Easter 4

| Year 1 | James 1: 17–21 | John 16: 5–15 |
| Year 2 | 1 John 3: 18–24 | John 5: 1–8 |

Almighty God, you alone can order the unruly wills and passions of sinful men: grant that your people may love what you command and desire what you promise so that among the many and varied changes of this world our hearts may be firmly fixed where true joys are to be found through Jesus Christ our Lord. **Amen.**

Easter 5

| Year 1 | James 1: 22–27 | John 16: 23–33 |
| Year 2 | 1 John 4: 7–10 | John 15: 9–17 |

O Lord, from whom all good things come, grant to us your servants that by your holy inspiration we may think good thoughts and by your merciful guidance put them into practice through our Lord Jesus Christ. **Amen.**

Ascension Day

| Year 1 | Acts 1: 1–11 | Mark 16: 14–20 |
| Year 2 | Acts 1: 1–11 | Luke 24: 46–53 |

Almighty God, we believe that your only begotten Son ascended into heaven: grant that in our hearts and minds we may also ascend there and dwell continually with him, who lives and reigns with you and the Holy Spirit, one God, for ever and ever. **Amen.**

Sunday after Ascension Day

Year 1   1 Peter 4: 7–11   John 15: 26–16: 4
Year 2   1 John 4: 11–16   John 17: 11b–19

O God, the King of glory, who exalted your only Son
Jesus Christ with great triumph to your kingdom in
heaven, do not leave us desolate, but send your Holy
Spirit to strengthen and exalt us to the place where our
Saviour Christ has gone before, who lives and reigns
with you and the Holy Spirit, one God, for ever. **Amen.**

Whit-Sunday (Pentecost)

Year 1   Acts 2: 1–11   John 14: 15–31
Year 2   1 Corinthians 12: 1–13   John 20: 19–23

Almighty God, who taught the hearts of your faithful
people by sending to them the light of your Holy
Spirit, grant that by the same Spirit we may judge
everything rightly and always rejoice in his holy
protection through the merits of Christ Jesus our
Saviour, who lives and reigns with you and the Holy
Spirit, one God, now and for ever. **Amen.**

Trinity Sunday

Year 1   Revelation 4: 1–11   John 3: 1–16
Year 2   Romans 8: 14–17   Matthew 28: 16–20

Almighty and everlasting God, you have given us grace,
thereby enabling us to bear witness to the glory of the
eternal Trinity and to worship you as the one God: we
humbly pray that you will keep us firm in the confession
of this faith and always defend us when we are in
trouble, for you live and reign the one true God. **Amen.**

Trinity 1

| Year 1 | 1 John 4: 7–21 | Luke 16: 19–31 |
| Year 2 | 1 Corinthians 7: 29–31 | Mark 1: 14–20 |

Lord God, the strength of all who put their trust in you, mercifully accept our prayers and, because through the weakness of our human nature we cannot do anything good without you, grant us the help of your grace so that in keeping your commandments we may please you both in will and deed through Jesus Christ our Lord. **Amen.**

Trinity 2

| Year 1 | 1 John 3: 13–24 | Luke 14: 16–24 |
| Year 2 | 2 Corinthians 5: 14–21 | Mark 4: 35–41 |

Lord God, the unfailing helper and guide of those whom you bring up in your unmovable fear and love, keep us, we pray, under the protection of your good providence and give us a continual reverence and love for your holy name, through Jesus Christ our Lord. **Amen.**

Trinity 3

| Year 1 | 1 Peter 5: 5–11 | Luke 15: 1–10 |
| Year 2 | Hebrews 4: 12–13 | Mark 10: 17–30 |

Graciously hear us, Lord God, and grant that we, to whom you have given the desire to pray, may be defended by your mighty aid and strengthened in all dangers and adversities, through Jesus Christ our Lord. **Amen.**

Trinity 4

Year 1	Romans 8: 18–23	Luke 6: 36–42
Year 2	Ephesians 4: 1–6	John 6: 1–15

Almighty God, the protector of all who believe in you and without whom nothing is strong, nothing is holy: increase and multiply upon us your mercy, that with you as our ruler and guide, we may pass through the things of this age in such a way that we do not finally lose the things of the age to come. Grant this, heavenly Father, for our Lord Jesus Christ's sake. **Amen.**

Trinity 5

Year 1	1 Peter 3: 8–15a	Luke 5: 1–11
Year 2	1 Thessalonians 5: 16–24	John 1: 19–28

Almighty God, we pray that you may so govern the course of this world that it may be peaceably ordered and that your church may joyfully serve you in all godly quietness, through Jesus Christ our Lord. **Amen.**

Trinity 6

Year 1	Romans 6: 3–11	Matthew 5: 20–26
Year 2	Ephesians 5: 15–20	John 6: 51–58

God our Father, you have prepared for those who love you good things that surpass our understanding: pour into our hearts such love towards you that, loving you above all, we may obtain your promises which are greater than we can desire, through Jesus Christ our Lord. **Amen.**

Trinity 7

Year 1   Romans 6: 19–23   Mark 8: 1–10
Year 2   Ephesians 1: 3–14   Mark 6: 7–13

Lord of all power and might, the author and giver of all good things, graft the love of your name in our hearts, increase in us true religion, nourish us with all that is good, and by your great mercy keep us in this condition, through Jesus Christ our Lord. **Amen.**

Trinity 8

Year 1   Romans 8: 12–17   Matthew 7: 15–23
Year 2   2 Corinthians 4: 6–12   Mark 2: 23–3: 6

Almighty God, whose never-failing providence governs everything in heaven and on earth, humbly we ask you to remove all that is hurtful and to give that which is profitable to us, through Jesus Christ our Lord. **Amen.**

Trinity 9

Year 1   1 Corinthians 10: 1–13   Luke 16: 1–9
Year 2   2 Corinthians 1: 18–22   Mark 2: 1–12

Grant us, Lord, we pray, the spirit always to think and do those things that are right, so that we, who cannot do anything good without you, may be able in your strength to live according to your will, through Jesus Christ our Lord. **Amen.**

Trinity 10

Year 1	1 Corinthians 12: 1–11	Luke 19: 41–48
Year 2	1 Corinthians 10: 31–11: 1	Mark 1: 40–45

Let your merciful ears, Lord God, be open to the prayers of your people and, so that we may obtain our petitions, teach us to ask for those things that please you, through Jesus Christ our Lord. **Amen.**

Trinity 11

Year 1	1 Corinthians 15: 1–11	Luke 18: 9–14
Year 2	James 5: 1–6	Mark 9: 38–48

Lord God, you show your Almighty power most of all in showing mercy and pity: grant us such a measure of your grace that in carrying out your commandments we may obtain your promises and share in your heavenly treasure, through Jesus Christ our Lord. **Amen.**

Trinity 12

Year 1	2 Corinthians 3: 4–11	Mark 7: 31–37
Year 2	James 1: 17–27	Mark 7: 1–23

Almighty and everlasting God, you are always more ready to hear than we are to pray and you constantly give more than we desire or deserve: pour down upon us the abundance of your mercy by forgiving us those things of which our consciences are afraid and by giving us those good things for which we are not worthy to ask except through the merits and mediation of Jesus Christ, your Son, our Lord. **Amen.**

Trinity 13

Year 1   Galatians 3: 16–22   Luke 10: 23–37
Year 2   Hebrews 7: 23–28   Mark 12: 28–34

Merciful God, by whose gift alone your faithful people offer you true and acceptable service, grant that we may serve you faithfully so that we do not finally fail to obtain your heavenly promises, through the merits of Jesus Christ our Lord. **Amen.**

Trinity 14

Year 1   Galatians 5: 16–24   Luke 17: 11–19
Year 2   Hebrews 5: 1–10   Mark 10: 46–52

Almighty and eternal God, grant that we may grow in faith, hope, and love; and, so that we may obtain what you promise, make us love what you command, through Jesus Christ our Lord. **Amen.**

Trinity 15

Year 1   Galatians 6: 11–18   Matthew 6: 24–34
Year 2   2 Corinthians 3: 1–6   Mark 2: 18–22

Guard your church, Lord God, with your continual mercy, and because in our frailty we cannot stand without you, keep us from all that may harm, and lead us to all that makes for our salvation, through Jesus Christ our Lord. **Amen.**

Trinity 16

Year 1   Ephesians 3: 13–21   Luke 7: 11–17
Year 2   James 3: 16–4: 3   Mark 9: 30–37

Lord, let your continual pity cleanse and defend your church, and because it cannot continue in safety without your aid, protect it by your help and goodness for ever, through Jesus Christ our Lord. **Amen.**

Trinity 17

Year 1   Ephesians 4: 1–6   Luke 14: 1–11
Year 2   2 Corinthians 5: 6–10   Mark 4: 26–34

Lord, we pray that your grace may always go before and follow after us and make us continually committed to all good works, through Jesus Christ our Lord. **Amen.**

Trinity 18

Year 1   1 Corinthians 1: 4–9   Matthew 22: 34–46
Year 2   2 Corinthians 12: 7–10   Mark 6: 1–6

Lord, give grace to your people to withstand the temptations of the world, the flesh, and the devil, and to follow you the only God with pure hearts and minds, through Jesus Christ our Lord. **Amen.**

Trinity 19

Year 1   Ephesians 4: 17–32   Matthew 9: 1–8
Year 2   2 Corinthians 4: 13–5: 5   Mark 3: 20–35

Lord God, because without you we are not able to please you: mercifully grant that your Holy Spirit may in everything direct and rule our hearts, through Jesus Christ our Lord. **Amen.**

Trinity 20

Year 1 Ephesians 5: 15–21   Matthew 22: 1–14
Year 2 Hebrews 9: 24–28   Mark 12: 38–44

Almighty and merciful God, keep us by your bountiful goodness from everything that may hurt us so that we may be ready both in body and soul cheerfully to accomplish whatever you want us to do, through Jesus Christ our Lord. **Amen.**

Trinity 21

Year 1 Ephesians 6: 10–20   John 4: 46–54
Year 2 James 2: 14–26   Mark 8: 27–35

Merciful Lord, grant to your faithful people pardon and peace that we may be cleansed from all our sins and serve you with a quiet mind, through Jesus Christ our Lord. **Amen.**

Trinity 22

Year 1 Philippians 1: 3–11   Matthew 18: 21–35
Year 2 Hebrews 10: 11–18   Mark 13: 24–32

Father in heaven, keep your household the church firm in godliness, so that it may by your protection be free from all adversities and may devoutly serve you in good works to the glory of your name, through Jesus Christ our Lord. **Amen.**

Trinity 23

Year 1	Philippians 3: 17–21	Matthew 22: 15–22
Year 2	1 Corinthians 9: 16–23	Mark 1: 29–39

Lord God, our refuge and strength, the author of all godliness, hear the devout prayers of your church and grant that what we ask for in faith we may surely obtain, through Jesus Christ our Lord. **Amen.**

Trinity 24

Year 1	Colossians 1: 3–14	Matthew 9: 18–26
Year 2	James 2: 1–5	Mark 7: 31–37

Lord, we pray, absolve your people from their offences so that through your bountiful goodness we may be set free from the chains of those sins which in our frailty we have committed; grant this, heavenly Father, for the sake of Jesus Christ, our Lord and Saviour. **Amen.**

Trinity 25 (*Sunday before Advent*)

Year 1	Jeremiah 23: 5–8	John 6: 5–14
Year 2	Revelation 1: 4–8	John 18: 33–37

Stir up the wills of your faithful people, Lord, so that we may produce abundantly the fruit of good works and receive your abundant reward, through Jesus Christ our Lord. **Amen.**

(If there are any more Sundays before Advent the collects for those Sundays after the Epiphany that were omitted are to be used. If there are fewer the surplus should be omitted providing that this collect for Trinity 25 is always used on the Sunday before Advent)

SAINTS' DAYS

Andrew (*30 November*)
Romans 10: 8–21   Matthew 4: 18–22

Almighty God, who gave such grace to your holy
apostle Andrew that he readily obeyed the call of your
Son Jesus Christ and followed him without delay, grant
that we who are called by your holy Word may give
ourselves at once to obey all your commands, through
Jesus Christ our Lord. **Amen.**

Thomas the apostle (*21 December*)
Ephesians 2: 19–22   John 20: 24–31

Almighty and eternal God, who permitted your holy
apostle Thomas to doubt your Son's resurrection to the
intent that the certainty of that event would be all the
more confirmed, grant that we may perfectly and
without any doubt believe in your Son Jesus Christ so
that our faith may never be found wanting in your
sight, through Jesus Christ, to whom with you and the
Holy Spirit be all glory, now and for ever. **Amen.**

Stephen (*26 December*)
Acts 7: 55–60   Matthew 23: 34–39

Grant, O Lord, that in all our sufferings for the
testimony of your truth we may look up steadfastly to
heaven and see by faith the glory that is to be revealed
and, filled with the Holy Spirit, may learn to love and
pray for our persecutors as Stephen your first martyr
prayed for his murderers to you, blessed Jesus, where

you stand at the right hand of God to help all who
suffer for you, our only mediator and advocate. **Amen.**

John the evangelist (*27 December*)
1 John 1: 1–10   John 21: 19*b*–25

Merciful Lord, let the bright beams of your light shine
upon your church so that, enlightened by the teaching
of your blessed apostle and evangelist John, we may
walk in the light of your truth and come at the last
to the light of eternal life, through Jesus Christ our
Lord. **Amen.**

The Innocents (*28 December*)
Revelation 14: 1–5   Matthew 2: 13–18

Almighty God, whose purpose it is that the lips of
children and infants praise you and who were glorified
in their deaths, put to death all evil within us and so
strengthen us by your grace that by the innocency of
our lives and constancy of our faith we may glorify
your holy name, through Jesus Christ our Lord. **Amen.**

The Conversion of Paul (*25 January*)
Acts 9: 1–22   Matthew 19: 27–30

O God, who through the preaching of the apostle Paul
caused the light of the gospel to shine throughout the
world, grant that as we remember his wonderful
conversion we may show our thankfulness by
following the holy doctrine which he taught, through
Jesus Christ our Lord. **Amen.**

The Presentation of Christ (*Purification of Mary*) (*2 February*)
Malachi 3: 1–5   Luke 2: 22–40

Almighty and everliving God, we humbly pray that as
your only Son was presented in the temple in our
human flesh, may we be presented to you with pure
and clean hearts by the same, your Son Jesus Christ our
Lord. **Amen.**

Matthias (*24 February*)
Acts 1: 15–26   Matthew 11: 25–30

Almighty God, who chose your faithful servant
Matthias to be numbered among the twelve apostles in
the place of Judas, grant that your church may always
be preserved from false apostles and guided by faithful
and true pastors, through Jesus Christ our Lord. **Amen.**

The Annunciation of Mary the virgin (*25 March*)
Isaiah 7: 10–15   Luke 1: 26–38

Pour your grace into our hearts O Lord we pray, so that,
as we have known the incarnation of your Son Jesus
Christ by the message of an angel, we may be brought
by his cross and suffering to the glory of his resurrection,
through the same Jesus Christ our Lord. **Amen.**

Mark (*25 April*)
Ephesians 4: 7–16   John 15: 1–11

Almighty God, who through the heavenly teaching of
Mark the evangelist instructed your church, give us

grace so that we may not be carried away with every
wind of false teaching but may be established in the
truth of your holy gospel, through Jesus Christ our
Lord. **Amen.**

Philip and James (*1 May*)
James 1: 1–12   John 14: 1–14

Almighty God, whom truly to know is eternal life,
grant us perfectly to know your Son Jesus Christ to be
the way, the truth, and the life, so that, following in
the steps of your holy apostles Philip and James, we
may steadfastly walk in the way that leads to eternal
life, through Jesus Christ your Son our Lord. **Amen.**

Barnabas the apostle (*11 June*)
Acts 11: 22–30   John 15: 12–17

Lord God Almighty, who endowed your holy apostle
Barnabas with special gifts of the Holy Spirit, do not
leave us destitute of your many gifts, nor of grace
always to use them to your honour and glory, through
Jesus Christ our Lord. **Amen.**

John the Baptist (*24 June*)
Isaiah 40: 1–11   Luke 1: 57–80

Almighty God, by whose providence your servant John
the Baptist was wonderfully born and sent to prepare
the way for your Son our Saviour by preaching
repentance, make us so to follow his teaching and the
example of his holy life that we may truly repent,

constantly speak the truth, boldly rebuke vice, and patiently suffer for the truth's sake, through Jesus Christ our Lord. **Amen.**

Peter (*29 June*)
Acts 12: 1–11   Matthew 16: 13–19

Almighty God, who by your Son Jesus Christ gave to your apostle Peter many excellent gifts and commanded him earnestly to feed your flock, make all bishops and pastors diligently to preach your word and all people obediently to follow it that they may receive the crown of eternal glory, through Jesus Christ our Lord. **Amen.**

James the apostle (*25 July*)
Acts 11: 27–12: 3   Matthew 20: 20–28

Grant, O merciful God, that as your holy apostle James left his father and all that he had and without delay obeyed the call of your Son Jesus Christ and followed him, so may we always be ready to forsake all worldly affections and follow your holy commands, through Jesus Christ our Lord. **Amen.**

Bartholomew the apostle (*24 August*)
Acts 5: 12–16   Luke 22: 24–30

Almighty and eternal God, who gave your apostle Bartholomew grace truly to believe and to preach your word, grant that your church may not only receive that word but also love and preach it, through Jesus Christ our Lord. **Amen.**

Matthew the apostle (*21 September*)
2 Corinthians 4: 1–6   Matthew 9: 9–13

Almighty God, who by your beloved Son did call
Matthew from his place of business to be an apostle
and evangelist, grant us grace to forsake all covetous
desires and the selfish love of riches and to follow your
Son Jesus Christ who lives and reigns with you and the
Holy Spirit, one God, now and for ever. **Amen.**

Michael and all angels (*29 September*)
Revelation 12: 7–12   Matthew 18: 1–11

Eternal God, by whom the ministries of angels and
men have been ordained and constituted in a
wonderful order, grant that as your holy angels always
serve you in heaven so by your appointment they may
help and defend us here on earth, through Jesus Christ
our Lord. **Amen.**

Luke the evangelist (*18 October*)
2 Timothy 4: 5–15   Luke 10: 1–7

Almighty God, who called Luke the physician to be an
evangelist and physician of the soul, praised by all the
churches for his service to the gospel, grant that through
the wholesome medicine of your word written by him
all the diseases of our souls may be healed, through the
merits of your Son Jesus Christ our Lord. **Amen.**

The apostles Simon and Jude (*28 October*)
Jude 1–8   John 15: 17–27

Almighty God, who built your church on the
foundation of the apostles and prophets, with Jesus
Christ as the chief cornerstone, grant us so to be joined
together in unity of spirit by their teaching that we
may be made a holy temple acceptable to you, through
Jesus Christ our Lord. **Amen.**

All saints (*1 November*)
Revelation 7: 2–12   Matthew 5: 1–12

Almighty God, who joined together your elect in one
communion and fellowship in the mystical body of
your Son Christ our Lord, grant us grace so to follow
your blessed saints in all virtuous and godly living that
we may come to those inexpressible joys that you have
prepared for those who sincerely love you, through
Jesus Christ our Lord. **Amen.**

Family Worship

1   *The minister announces the opening* HYMN.

2   *This* CONFESSION *is said:*

Minister   If we claim to be without sin, we deceive ourselves and
           the truth is not in us. *1 John 1: 8*
All   **If we confess our sins, God is faithful and just and
           will forgive us our sins and purify us from all
           unrighteousness.** *1 John 1: 9*

Minister   Let us confess our sins to Almighty God.
All   **Almighty and most merciful Father,
           we have strayed from you like lost sheep.
           We have followed our own ways,
           and have broken your holy laws.
           We have left undone what we ought to have done,
           and have done what we ought not to have done.
           We cannot save ourselves.
           O Lord have mercy on us pitiful sinners.
           Restore those who truly repent,
           as you have promised through Jesus Christ our Lord.
           And grant that we may live a holy life,
           to the glory of your name. Amen.**

3   *The minister prays for* GOD'S FORGIVENESS, *saying:*

           Merciful Lord, grant to your faithful people pardon and
           peace that we may be cleansed from all our sins and
           serve you with a quiet mind, through Jesus Christ our
           Lord. **Amen.**

4   THE LORD'S PRAYER:

	either	*or*

All   **Our Father who art in
            heaven,
        hallowed be thy name,
        thy kingdom come,
        thy will be done,
        on earth as it is in heaven.
        Give us this day
        our daily bread.
        And forgive us our
            trespasses
        as we forgive those
        who trespass against us.
        And lead us not into
            temptation
        but deliver us from evil.
        For thine is the kingdom,
        the power, and the glory,
        for ever and ever. Amen.**

**Our Father in heaven,
hallowed be your name,
your kingdom come,
your will be done,
on earth as it is in heaven.
Give us today
our daily bread.
Forgive us our sins
as we forgive those
who sin against us.
Lead us not into
    temptation
but deliver us from evil.
For yours is the kingdom,
the power, and the glory,
now and for ever. Amen.**

5   *We stand to sing a* PSALM, HYMN, *or* SONG.

6   A BIBLE READING *follows, after which the reader says:*

        This is the word of the Lord.
All   **Thanks be to God.**

7   THE NOTICES *and* BANNS OF MARRIAGE *are announced, after
        which the* OFFERING *is brought forward and received.*

8   A HYMN *or* SONG *may be sung.*

9   THE APOSTLES' CREED. *This may be said either straight
through, or one paragraph at a time in response to the questions
in brackets.*

(Minister Do you believe in God the Father?)

All   **I believe in God, the Father Almighty,
          Creator of heaven and earth.**

(Minister Do you believe in the Lord Jesus Christ?)

All   **I believe in Jesus Christ,
          his only Son, our Lord.
          He was conceived by the Holy Spirit
          and born of the virgin Mary.
          He suffered under Pontius Pilate,
          was crucified, died, and was buried.
          He descended to the dead.
          On the third day he rose again.
          He ascended into heaven,
          and sits at the right hand of the Father.
          From there he shall come again
          to judge the living and the dead.**

(Minister Do you believe in the Holy Spirit?)

All   **I believe in the Holy Spirit,
          the holy catholic church,
          the communion of saints,
          the forgiveness of sins,
          the resurrection of the body,
          and the life everlasting. Amen.**

10   *Any special* ACTIVITY *follows, then a* SONG.

11   THE SERMON *is preached.*

12   THE COLLECT *(special prayer)* OF THE DAY *(pp. 84 ff.).*

13   *Other* PRAYERS *(see e.g. pp. 39 ff.). These may end with*
           THE GRACE:

All   **The grace of our Lord Jesus Christ,**
           and the love of God,
           and the fellowship of the Holy Spirit,
           be with us all evermore. Amen.

14   A HYMN *is sung.*

15   *The minister dismisses the people with a* PRAYER *or* BLESSING.

Thanksgiving for the Birth of a Child

1   *The minister says:*

Give thanks to the Lord, call on his name;
make known among the nations what he has done.
Psalm 105: 1

Almighty God, of his great goodness, has been pleased to
keep *N* safe in childbirth and has given her *and N a son,
N*. Let us therefore give heartfelt thanks to God.

2   A PSALM *is said or sung by all.*

PSALM 116 (verses 1, 2, 5, 7, 12–14, 17–19)

I love the Lord, for he heard my voice:
he heard my cry for mercy.
Because he turned his ear to me,
I will call on him as long as I live.

The Lord is gracious and righteous;
our God is full of compassion.

Be at rest once more, O my soul,
for the Lord has been good to you.

How can I repay the Lord
for all his goodness to me?
I will lift up the cup of salvation
and call on the name of the Lord.
I will fulfil my vows to the Lord
in the presence of all his people.

I will sacrifice a thank-offering to you
and call on the name of the Lord.
I will fulfil my vows to the Lord
in the presence of all his people,
in the courts of the house of the Lord—
in your midst, O Jerusalem.

Praise the Lord.

or

PSALM 127

Unless the Lord builds the house,
its builders labour in vain.
Unless the Lord watches over the city,
the watchmen stand guard in vain.
In vain you rise early and stay up late,
toiling for food to eat—
for he grants sleep to those he loves.

Sons are a heritage from the Lord,
children a reward from him.
Like arrows in the hands of a warrior
are sons born in one's youth.
Blessed is the man whose quiver is full of them.
They will not be put to shame
when they contend with their enemies in the gate.

3   THE PRAYERS

Minister   Let us pray.
           Lord, have mercy upon us.
All   **Christ, have mercy upon us.**
Minister   Lord, have mercy upon us.

THE LORD'S PRAYER:

either	*or*
Our Father who art in heaven, **hallowed be thy name,** **thy kingdom come,** **thy will be done,** **on earth as it is in heaven.** **Give us this day** **our daily bread.** **And forgive us our trespasses** **as we forgive those who trespass against us.** **And lead us not into temptation** **but deliver us from evil.** **For thine is the kingdom,** **the power, and the glory,** **for ever and ever. Amen.**	**Our Father in heaven,** **hallowed be your name,** **your kingdom come,** **your will be done,** **on earth as it is in heaven.** **Give us today** **our daily bread.** **Forgive us our sins** **as we forgive those who sin against us.** **Lead us not into temptation** **but deliver us from evil.** **For yours is the kingdom,** **the power, and the glory,** **now and for ever. Amen.**

All (*above both columns*)

Minister   O Lord, save *these* your *servants*;
All   **and all who put their trust in you.**
Minister   Be to *them* a strong tower;
All   **and *their* refuge and strength.**
Minister   My soul praises the Lord,
All   **and my spirit rejoices in God my Saviour.**
Minister   Lord, hear our prayer.
All   **And let our cry come to you. Amen.**

The minister continues in prayer, saying:

Almighty God, we give you humble thanks because you have been pleased to keep *N* safe through childbirth and to give *these* your *servants a son*. Grant, we pray, most merciful Father, that *they* may walk with you; be faithful in teaching *their* child the Christian way of life; and that in the life to come *they* may enjoy eternal glory through Jesus Christ our Lord. **Amen.**

Infant Baptism

First Order

1   *The minister says these words of* EXHORTATION:

The Scriptures teach that all people are conceived and
born with a sinful nature; and because our Saviour
Christ says that no one can enter the kingdom of God
unless he is born of water and the Holy Spirit, I ask you
to call upon God, in the name of the Lord Jesus Christ,
to have mercy on *this child* and to give *him* that which by
nature *he* cannot have, namely, that *he* may be baptized
with water and the Holy Spirit, received into Christ's
holy church, and made *a* living *member* of the same.

2   *The minister says:*

Let us pray.

All   **Almighty and eternal God,**
who in mercy saved Noah and his family
in the days of the flood,
and who safely led the children of Israel
through the waters of the Red Sea,
symbolizing thereby holy baptism;
and by the baptism of your Son, Jesus Christ,
sanctified water to represent the washing away of
**   sin:**
look in mercy on *this child.*
Wash *him,* **and sanctify** *him* **with the Holy Spirit;**
deliver *him* **from your wrath;**

receive *him* into the ark of Christ's church;
make *him* firm in faith and joyful through hope;
and fill *him* with your love so that,
passing through the waters of this troubled world,
he may finally come to the land of everlasting life,
there to reign with you for ever,
through Jesus Christ our Lord. Amen.

Almighty God, our heavenly Father,
you give aid to the needy, strength to the helpless,
and eternal life to those who believe.
Grant to *this child*, who *comes* to be baptized,
forgiveness of sins and spiritual regeneration.
According to your promise receive *him*,
and make *him an heir* of eternal salvation;
through Jesus Christ our Lord. Amen.

3   *The minister reads these words from the Gospel of Mark:*

Hear these words of our Lord Jesus Christ as recorded
in the tenth chapter of Mark's Gospel, verses 13–16:

   People were bringing little children to Jesus to have
him touch them, but the disciples rebuked them.
When Jesus saw this, he was indignant. He said to
them, 'Let the little children come to me, and do not
hinder them, for the kingdom of God belongs to such
as these. I tell you the truth, anyone who will not
receive the kingdom of God like a little child will never
enter it.' And he took the children in his arms, put his
hands upon them, and blessed them.

4   *The minister continues:*

You hear in these words that our Saviour Christ invites
children to be brought to him. He rebukes those who
keep them from him and he exhorts us to show
childlike trust. The way he embraced and blessed little
children teaches us that he is ready to receive all who
are brought to him. Be assured therefore that he, who
encouraged his followers to bring their children to
baptism, will receive, embrace, and give to them the
blessing of eternal life. Therefore we pray:

All   **Almighty God, our heavenly Father,**
we humbly thank you for calling us to know you
and for teaching us to trust in you:
increase this knowledge
and strengthen this faith.
Give your Holy Spirit to *this child,*
that *he* **may be born again**
and made *an heir* **of eternal salvation,**
through Jesus Christ our Lord,
who lives and reigns with you and the Holy Spirit,
now and for ever. Amen.

5   *The minister invites the parent(s) and godparents to stand, and*
says these words to them:

You have brought *this child* to be baptized. You have
prayed that our Lord Jesus Christ will receive *him*,
forgive *him*, sanctify *him* with the Holy Spirit, and
make *him an heir* to heaven and eternal life. You have
heard also that our Lord has promised all these things
in his gospel and we know that he keeps his promises.
   At baptism we promise to reject the devil and all evil,

constantly to believe God's Word, and to obey his commands. Children should make their own response of faith and obedience towards God, but as *this child is* at present too young to answer for *himself* it is proper that this commitment be made in *his* name until *he is* old enough to take it upon *himself*. I ask therefore:

Do you, in the name of *this child*, renounce the devil and all his works, the empty show and false values of the world, and the sinful desires of the flesh, so that you will not follow nor be led by them?

Answer **I renounce them all.**

Minister   Do you believe in God, the Father Almighty, Maker of heaven and earth?

Do you believe in Jesus Christ, his one and only Son, our Lord? And that he was conceived by the Holy Spirit, born of the virgin Mary; that he suffered under Pontius Pilate, was crucified, dead, and buried; that he went down to the dead, and also rose again the third day; that he ascended into heaven and sits at the right hand of God the Father Almighty; and from there shall come again at the end of the world to judge the living and the dead?

And do you believe in the Holy Spirit, the holy catholic church, the communion of saints, the forgiveness of sins, the resurrection of the body, and eternal life after death?

Answer **All this I firmly believe.**

Minister   Do you in the name of *this child* desire baptism?
Answer **That is my desire.**

Minister   Will you then obey God's commands and serve him faithfully all the days of your life?
Answer **I will, with the help of God.**

6   *The minister says:*

Let us pray.

Merciful God, grant that the old Adam in *this child* may
be buried, and that *he* may be raised *a* new *man* in
Christ. **Amen.**

Grant that the sinful desires of the flesh may die in *him*,
and that all things belonging to the Spirit may live and
grow in *him*. **Amen.**

Grant that by faith *he* may have power and strength to
have victory and to triumph over the devil, the world,
and the flesh. **Amen.**

Almighty God, whose Son Jesus Christ shed from his
side both water and blood for the forgiveness of our
sins; and commanded his disciples to go and teach all
nations baptizing them in the name of the Father, and
of the Son, and of the Holy Spirit: hear our prayer.
Consecrate this water to signify the washing away
of sin; and grant that *this child* now to be baptized in it,
may receive the fullness of your grace and be numbered
among your chosen and believing children, through
Jesus Christ our Lord. **Amen.**

7   *The minister baptizes the child with water, first saying to the
parent(s) and godparents:*

Name this child.

N, I baptize you in the name of the Father,
and of the Son, and of the Holy Spirit. **Amen.**

8   THE CHARGE

We receive you into
the congregation of Christ's flock
and sign you with the sign of the cross.
We pray that you will not be ashamed
to confess the faith of Christ crucified.

All   **Fight bravely under his banner**
against sin, the world, and the devil,
and continue Christ's faithful *soldier*
and *servant* **to the end of your** *life.* **Amen.**

9   *The minister continues:*

Now that *this child is* a baptized member of the
Christian church, let us give thanks to God and pray
that *he* will live the rest of *his life* according to this
beginning.

10   THE LORD'S PRAYER:

either	*or*

All   **Our Father who art in**
      heaven,
hallowed be thy name,
thy kingdom come,
thy will be done,
on earth as it is in heaven.
Give us this day
our daily bread.
And forgive us our
    trespasses
as we forgive those
who trespass against us.
	Our Father in heaven,
	hallowed be your name,
	your kingdom come,
	your will be done,
	on earth as it is in heaven.
	Give us today
	our daily bread.
	Forgive us our sins
	as we forgive those
	who sin against us.
	Lead us not into
	    temptation

And lead us not into
temptation
but deliver us from evil.
For thine is the kingdom,
the power, and the glory,
for ever and ever. Amen.

but deliver us from evil.
For yours is the kingdom,
the power, and the glory,
now and for ever. Amen.

11   *Then the minister says:*

We praise you, most merciful Father, that all whom
you receive and adopt as your own are spiritually
regenerate and made true members of your church;
and we pray you to grant that *this child*, being buried
and raised with Christ, may have victory over sin, the
world, and the devil, that *he* may live *a* righteous *life*,
and that at the end *he* may inherit your eternal
kingdom along with all your faithful people, through
Jesus Christ our Lord. **Amen.**

12   *The minister addresses the parent(s) and godparents:*

It is now your duty as parent(*s*) and godparents to see
that *this child is* taught, as soon as *he is* able to learn,
the promises you have made in *his* name. And it is
your responsibility to ensure that *he is* taught the
Christian faith and what it means to trust in Christ.

To this end you should bring *him* to church to receive
instruction in God's Word, and in particular you
should see that *he is* taught the Lord's prayer, the ten
commandments, the creed, and the catechism. You are
to encourage *him* to lead a godly, Christian life and to
follow the example of our Lord and Saviour Jesus
Christ. And you are to ensure that, when old enough,

he publicly *confirms his* baptismal promises in the
presence of the bishop.

13   *The minister may conclude with the* GRACE:

The grace of our Lord Jesus Christ,
and the love of God,
and the fellowship of the Holy Spirit,
be with us all evermore. **Amen.**

Infant Baptism

Second Order

1 THE INTRODUCTION

The minister reads this introduction:

The Lord Jesus Christ said: All authority in heaven and on earth has been given to me. Therefore go and make disciples of all nations, baptizing them in the name of the Father and of the Son and of the Holy Spirit, and teaching them to obey everything I have commanded you. *Matthew 28: 18–20*

Since the time of Abraham God's people have been given a sign of admission to his covenant by means of which God reassures his children that he is their God and they his people. In the New Testament baptism replaced circumcision as the sign, but the covenant itself remains the same. Those who believe God's promise and trust in Christ alone for salvation, are made the spiritual heirs of Abraham and the children of God.

Baptism signifies that, as water washes away dirt, so Christ's blood washes away sin. This blessing of cleansing from sin, along with new birth by the Holy Spirit, union with Christ, and renewed spiritual life are promised to believers and their children, as Peter made clear when he said: The promise is for you and your children, and for all who are afar off—for all whom the Lord our God will call. *Acts 2: 39*

We read in the Gospels of the love Christ has for the children of the covenant and of his readiness to bless them. The Lord Jesus Christ is always the same. His promises are sure. But because we are all conceived and born with sinful natures, and our Saviour Christ says: No one can enter the kingdom of God unless he is born of water and the Holy Spirit (*John 3: 5*), I urge you to call upon God the Father in the name of the Lord Jesus Christ that, by his infinite mercy he will give to *this child* what by nature *he* cannot have, namely, that *he* may be baptized with water and the Holy Spirit, received into Christ's holy church, and made *an* active *member* of the same.

2

All **Almighty and everlasting God,**
we ask you to have mercy on *this child*.
Fill *him* **with the Holy Spirit,**
give to *him* **a knowledge of the forgiveness of sin,**
deliver *him* **from your wrath,**
and grant that *he* **may grow in the fear and**
knowledge of the Lord Jesus Christ,
who lives and reigns with you and the Holy Spirit,
now and for ever. Amen.

3 THE DUTIES OF PARENTS AND GODPARENTS

The minister invites the parent(s) and godparents to stand and says:

The *child* you have brought to baptism *depends* chiefly on you for the help and encouragement *he needs*. I ask therefore:

Are you yourself a Christian, a follower of Jesus Christ, a member of his church, and one who sincerely believes the promises of God?

Answer   **I am.**

Minister   It is your duty to provide at every stage of *this child's* growth instruction in Christian doctrine. Especially you must teach *him* to trust in Christ alone as the only way to forgiveness and salvation. Are you willing to sponsor *this child*, to accept responsibility for *his* Christian upbringing, and to pray for *him* regularly?

Answer   **I am willing.**

4   THE DECLARATION OF REPENTANCE, FAITH, AND OBEDIENCE

The minister addresses the parent(s) and godparents:

Minister   *This child is* too young to profess repentance, faith, and obedience for *himself*. I therefore ask you to answer these questions on *his* behalf until *he is* old enough to speak for *himself*.

Do you renounce the devil and all his works, the empty show and false values of the world, and the sinful desires of the flesh, so that you will not follow nor be led by them?

Answer   **I renounce them all.**

Minister   Do you believe and trust in God, the Father Almighty,
Maker of heaven and earth, who loved the world so
much that he sent his Son to die for us?

Do you believe and trust in his only Son Jesus Christ,
who was crucified for our sins, rose from the dead, and
is the only way of salvation?

Do you believe and trust in his Holy Spirit, who
enables us to receive God's word, repent, and believe
the Gospel?

Answer   **I believe and trust in the one true God,
Father, Son, and Holy Spirit.**

Minister   Will you keep God's holy will and commandments all
the days of your life?

Answer   **I will, with the help of God.**

5

All   **O Lord our heavenly Father,
we thank you that by your infinite love and mercy,
you have made a covenant with us in your dear Son,
the Lord Jesus Christ,
in which you have promised that you will be our
God,
and we shall be your children.
Grant that** *this child*
may know you as *his* **heavenly Father,
and enter your kingdom through faith in your
beloved Son.
Grant** *him* **power, strength, and victory in Christ
over the world, the flesh, and the devil;
and, give** *him* **all spiritual blessings and grace
that** *he* **may ever live to your praise and glory,
through Jesus Christ our Lord. Amen.**

6   THE BAPTISM

The minister baptizes the child with water, first saying to the parent(s) and godparents:

Name this child.

N, I baptize you in the name of the Father,
and of the Son, and of the Holy Spirit. **Amen.**

7   THE CHARGE

We receive you into Christ's congregation,
and sign you with the sign of the cross.
We pray that you will not be ashamed
to confess the faith of Christ crucified.

All   **Fight bravely under his banner**
against sin, the world, and the devil;
and continue Christ's faithful *soldier*
and *servant* **to the end of your** *life*. **Amen.**

8   THE LORD'S PRAYER:

either

or

All   **Our Father who art in**
heaven,
hallowed be thy name,
thy kingdom come,
thy will be done,
on earth as it is in heaven.
Give us this day
our daily bread.
And forgive us our
trespasses

Our Father in heaven,
hallowed be your name,
your kingdom come,
your will be done,
on earth as it is in heaven.
Give us today
our daily bread.
Forgive us our sins
as we forgive those
who sin against us.

as we forgive those
who trespass against us.
And lead us not into
    temptation
but deliver us from evil.
For thine is the kingdom,
the power, and the glory,
for ever and ever. Amen.
	Lead us not into
	    temptation
	but deliver us from evil.
	For yours is the kingdom,
	the power, and the glory,
	now and for ever. Amen.

9 *All join in praying for the parent(s) and godparents:*

**Almighty God, our heavenly Father,
we pray for the parent(s) and godparents of** *this child.*
**Give to them spiritual wisdom and grace
that they may keep the vows which they have made
and bring up** *this child*
**in the fear and nurture of the Lord.
And grant that at the last they may receive
the eternal joys of heaven;
through Jesus Christ our Lord. Amen.**

10 *The minister addresses the parent(s) and godparents:*

It is your duty as parent(*s*) and godparents to see that *N
is* taught, as soon as *he is* able to learn, the promises
you have made in *his* name. And it is your
responsibility to ensure that *he is* taught the Christian
faith and what it means to trust in Christ. You must
encourage *him* to lead a godly, Christian life and to
follow the example of our Lord and Saviour Jesus
Christ. And you are to ensure that, when old enough,
he publicly *confirms his* baptismal promises.

11   *The minister may conclude with the* GRACE:

The grace of our Lord Jesus Christ,
and the love of God,
and the fellowship of the Holy Spirit,
be with us all evermore. **Amen.**

Adult Baptism

1   THE INTRODUCTION

The minister reads this introduction:

The Lord Jesus Christ said: All authority in heaven and
on earth has been given to me. Therefore go and make
disciples of all nations, baptizing them in the name of
the Father and of the Son and of the Holy Spirit, and
teaching them to obey everything I have commanded
you. *Matthew 28: 18–20*

Since the time of Abraham God's people have been given
a sign of admission to his covenant by means of which
God reassures his children that he is their God and they
his people. In the New Testament baptism replaced
circumcision as the sign, but the covenant itself
remains the same. Those who believe God's promise
and trust in Christ alone for salvation, are made the
spiritual heirs of Abraham and the children of God.

Our Lord Jesus Christ suffered death on the cross and
rose again from the dead for our salvation. Baptism is
the outward sign of all that God does for us in Christ.
He unites us with him in his death, grants us
forgiveness of sins for his sake, and raises us with
him to new life in the Spirit.

2   The minister says:

Let us pray.

Almighty and eternal God,
who in mercy saved Noah and his family
in the days of the flood,
and who safely led the children of Israel
through the waters of the Red Sea,
symbolizing thereby holy baptism;
and by the baptism of your Son, Jesus Christ,
sanctified water to represent the washing away of sin:
look in mercy on *this person.*
Wash *him,* and sanctify *him* with the Holy Spirit;
deliver *him* from your wrath;
receive *him* into the ark of Christ's church;
make *him* firm in faith and joyful through hope;
and fill *him* with your love so that,
passing through the waters of this troubled world,
he may finally come to the land of everlasting life,
there to reign with you for ever,
through Jesus Christ our Lord. **Amen.**

3   *The minister reads these words from the Gospel of John:*

Hear these words of our Lord Jesus Christ as recorded
in the third chapter of John's Gospel, verses 1–8:

Now there was a man of the Pharisees named
Nicodemus, a member of the Jewish ruling council. He
came to Jesus at night and said, 'Rabbi, we know you
are a teacher who has come from God. For no one
could perform the miraculous signs you are doing if
God were not with him.'

In reply Jesus declared, 'I tell you the truth, unless a
man is born again, he cannot see the kingdom of God.'

'How can a man be born when he is old?' Nicodemus
asked. 'Surely he cannot enter a second time into his
mother's womb to be born!'

Jesus answered, 'I tell you the truth, unless a man is born of water and the Spirit, he cannot enter the kingdom of God. Flesh gives birth to flesh, but the Spirit gives birth to spirit. You should not be surprised at my saying, "You must be born again." The wind blows wherever it pleases. You hear its sound, but you cannot tell where it comes from or where it is going. So it is with everyone born of the Spirit.'

4   THE DECLARATION OF REPENTANCE, FAITH, AND OBEDIENCE

The candidate(s) stand(s) and the minister says:

The Scriptures teach that all people are conceived and born with a sinful nature; and you have heard in these words of our Saviour Christ that no one can enter the kingdom of God unless he is born of water and the Holy Spirit. The sacramental sign of the new birth is baptism. Those who come to be baptized must affirm their allegiance to Christ and their rejection of all that displeases God. It is your duty to fight against evil and to follow Christ. Therefore I ask:

Do you renounce the devil and all his works, the empty show and false values of the world, and the sinful desires of the flesh, so that you will not follow nor be led by them?

Answer   **I renounce them all.**

Minister   Do you believe and trust in God, the Father Almighty, Maker of heaven and earth, who loved the world so much that he sent his Son to die for us?

Do you believe and trust in his only Son Jesus Christ,
who was crucified for our sins, rose from the dead, and
is the only way of salvation?

Do you believe and trust in his Holy Spirit, who
enables us to receive God's word, repent, and believe
the gospel?

Answer **I believe and trust in the one true God,
Father, Son, and Holy Spirit.**

Minister Do you desire to be baptized in this faith?
Answer **That is my desire.**

Minister Will you then keep God's holy will and commandments
all the days of your life?
Answer **I will, with the help of God.**

5 *The minister says:*

Let us pray.

Merciful God, grant that the old Adam in *this person* may
be buried, and that *he* may be raised *a* new *man* in
Christ. **Amen.**

Grant that the sinful desires of the flesh may die in
him, and that all things belonging to the Spirit may
live and grow in *him*. **Amen.**

Grant that by faith *he* may have power and strength
to have victory and to triumph over the devil, the
world, and the flesh. **Amen.**

Almighty God, whose Son Jesus Christ shed from his
side both water and blood for the forgiveness of our

sins; and commanded his disciples to go and teach all
nations baptizing them in the name of the Father, and
of the Son, and of the Holy Spirit: hear our prayer.
Consecrate this water to signify the washing away
of sin; and grant that *this person* now to be baptized in
it, may receive the fullness of your grace and be
numbered among your chosen and believing children,
through Jesus Christ our Lord. **Amen.**

6   THE BAPTISM

The minister baptizes the candidate with water, saying:

N, I baptize you in the name of the Father,
and of the Son, and of the Holy Spirit. **Amen.**

7   THE CHARGE

We receive you into Christ's congregation,
and sign you with the sign of the cross.
We pray that you will not be ashamed
to confess the faith of Christ crucified.

All   **Fight bravely under his banner
against sin, the world, and the devil;
and continue Christ's faithful soldier
and servant to the end of your life. Amen.**

8   THE LORD'S PRAYER:

either

All   Our Father who art in
      heaven,
      hallowed be thy name,
      thy kingdom come,
      thy will be done,
      on earth as it is in heaven.
      Give us this day
      our daily bread.
      And forgive us our
      trespasses
      as we forgive those
      who trespass against us.
      And lead us not into
      temptation
      but deliver us from evil.
      For thine is the kingdom,
      the power, and the glory,
      for ever and ever. Amen.

or

Our Father in heaven,
hallowed be your name,
your kingdom come,
your will be done,
on earth as it is in heaven.
Give us today
our daily bread.
Forgive us our sins
as we forgive those
who sin against us.
Lead us not into
temptation
but deliver us from evil.
For yours is the kingdom,
the power, and the glory,
now and for ever. Amen.

9   *Then the minister says:*

We praise you, most merciful Father, that all whom
you receive and adopt as your own are spiritually
regenerate and made true members of your church;
and we pray you to grant that *this person*, being buried
and raised with Christ, may have victory over sin, the
world, and the devil, that *he* may live *a* righteous *life*,
and that at the end *he* may inherit your eternal
kingdom along with all your faithful people, through
Jesus Christ our Lord. **Amen.**

10   *The minister addresses the newly baptized:*

You have today solemnly promised in the presence of
this congregation and your chosen witnesses that you
will follow Christ. It is your duty to trust in him, to
follow his example daily, and to be *a* faithful and loyal
member of his family, the church.

You should develop the habit of daily Bible reading
and prayer. And if you are not coming to confirmation
today you should as soon as possible be confirmed and
then regularly receive Holy Communion, by which we
are reminded of Christ's death for us and at which we
rededicate ourselves to his service.

11   *The minister may conclude with the* GRACE:

The grace of our Lord Jesus Christ,
and the love of God,
and the fellowship of the Holy Spirit,
be with us all evermore. **Amen.**

The Catechism

Q1   *What is your name?*
A   My name is . . .

Q2   *Who gave you this name?*
A   My parent(s) and godparents at my baptism. Through baptism I was made a member of Christ, the child of God, and an inheritor of the kingdom of heaven.

Q3   *What did your parent(s) and godparents do on your behalf at your baptism?*
A   They affirmed their allegiance to Christ, their rejection of all that is evil, and their resolve to fight against evil and to follow Christ. They affirmed all this in my name as well as their own.

Q4   *What does following Christ involve?*
A   It involves three things: first, renouncing the devil and all his works, the empty show and false values of the world, and the sinful desires of the flesh; secondly, believing all that the Bible teaches about the articles of the Christian faith; and thirdly, keeping God's holy will and commandments all the days of my life.

Q5   *Do you think yourself bound to do these things?*
A   Most certainly, with the Lord as my helper. I heartily thank God our heavenly Father that he has called me to the state of salvation through Jesus Christ our Saviour. And I pray that he will give me his grace to continue in this state to the end of my life.

Q6   *What do you believe?*
A   I believe in God, the Father Almighty,
Creator of heaven and earth.
   I believe in Jesus Christ,
his only Son, our Lord.
He was conceived by the Holy Spirit
and born of the virgin Mary.
He suffered under Pontius Pilate,
was crucified, died, and was buried.
He descended to the dead.
On the third day he rose again.
He ascended into heaven,
and sits at the right hand of the Father.
From there he will come again
to judge the living and the dead.
   I believe in the Holy Spirit,
the holy catholic church,
the communion of saints,
the forgiveness of sins,
the resurrection of the body,
and the life everlasting.

Q7   *What do you chiefly learn from the Apostles' Creed?*
A   First, I learn to believe in God the Father, who has
made me and all the world; secondly, in God the Son,
who has redeemed me and all mankind; thirdly, in God
the Holy Spirit, who sanctifies me and all the elect
people of God.

Q8   *How many commandments are there?*
A   Ten.

Q9   *What are they?*
A   They are found in Exodus, chapter 20, where we read
that God spoke all these words: I am the Lord your

God, who brought you out of Egypt, out of the land of slavery.

1 You shall have no gods other than me.
2 You shall not make for yourself an idol in the form of anything in heaven above or on the earth beneath or in the waters below. You shall not bow down to them nor worship them, for I, the Lord your God, am a jealous God who punishes the children for the sin of the fathers to the third and fourth generations of those who hate me, but I show love to thousands who love me and keep my commandments.
3 You shall not misuse the name of the Lord your God, for the Lord will not hold anyone guiltless who misuses his name.
4 Remember to keep the Sabbath day holy. Six days you shall labour and do all your work, but the seventh day is a Sabbath to the Lord your God. On it you shall not do any work, neither you nor your son or daughter, nor your manservant or maidservant, nor your animals, nor the foreigner living among you. For in six days the Lord made the heavens and the earth, the sea and all that is in them, but he rested on the seventh day. Therefore the Lord blessed the Sabbath day and made it holy.
5 Honour your father and your mother, so that you may live long in the land the Lord your God is giving you.
6 You shall not commit murder.
7 You shall not commit adultery.
8 You shall not steal.
9 You shall not bear false witness against your neighbour.
10 You shall not covet your neighbour's house. You shall not covet your neighbour's wife, nor his manservant, his maidservant, his ox or donkey, nor anything that belongs to him.

Q10   *What do you chiefly learn from these commandments?*
A   I learn two things: my duty to God and my duty to my neighbour.

Q11   *What is your duty to God?*
A   My duty to God is: to believe in him, to fear him, and to love him with all my heart, with all my mind, with all my soul, and with all my strength; to worship him, to give him thanks, to put my whole trust in him, to pray to him, to honour his holy name and his Word, and to serve him truly throughout my life.

Q12   *What is your duty to your neighbour?*
A   My duty to my neighbour is: to love him as myself and to do to all as I wish they would do to me; to love, honour, and care for my parents; to honour and obey the *Queen* and all in authority under *her*; to submit to my teachers and spiritual pastors; to be humble and show respect; to hurt no one by word or deed; to be true and just in all that I do; to bear no malice or hatred in my heart; to keep my hands from stealing and my tongue from evil speaking, lying, and slandering; to keep my body in temperance, sobriety, and chastity; not to covet nor desire other people's goods; but to learn to work honestly for my own living and to do my duty in that state of life to which it shall please God to call me.

Q13   *You are not able to do these things in your own strength, nor are you able to keep his commandments or serve him without his special grace. This you must learn at all times to call for by diligent prayer. Therefore recite the Lord's Prayer.*

A

Either

Our Father who art in
    heaven,
hallowed be thy name,
thy kingdom come,
thy will be done,
on earth as it is in heaven.
Give us this day
our daily bread.
And forgive us our
    trespasses
as we forgive those
    who trespass against us.
And lead us not into
    temptation
but deliver us from evil.
For thine is the kingdom,
the power, and the glory,
for ever and ever. Amen.

or

Our Father in heaven,
    hallowed be your name,
your kingdom come,
your will be done,
on earth as it is in heaven.
Give us today
our daily bread.
Forgive us our sins
as we forgive those
    who sin against us.
Lead us not into
    temptation
but deliver us from evil.
For yours is the kingdom,
the power, and the glory,
now and for ever. Amen.

Q14   *What do you ask God for in this prayer?*

A   I ask God our heavenly Father, the giver of all
goodness, to send his grace to me and to everyone, so
that we may worship him, serve him, and obey him as
we ought. And I pray God to send us all that we need
both for our souls and bodies; that he will show us
mercy and forgive us our sins; that he will be pleased
to save and defend us in all spiritual and bodily
dangers; and that he will keep us from all sin and
wickedness, from our spiritual enemy, and from
everlasting death. This I trust he will do out of his
mercy and goodness, through our Lord Jesus Christ.
And therefore I say, Amen, so be it.

Q15 *How many sacraments has Christ ordained in his church?*
A   Two only, as generally necessary to salvation: baptism and the Lord's Supper (or Holy Communion).

Q16 *What does the word sacrament mean?*
A   A sacrament is an outward and visible sign of an inward and spiritual grace, given to us, ordained by Christ himself, as a means by which we receive that grace and a pledge to assure us of it.

Q17 *How many parts are there to a sacrament?*
A   Two: the outward visible sign, and the inward spiritual grace.

Q18 *What is the outward visible sign in baptism?*
A   Water: in which a person is baptized in the name of the Father and of the Son and of the Holy Spirit.

Q19 *What is the inward and spiritual grace?*
A   Death to sin and new birth to righteousness; for being born with a sinful nature and being children of wrath, we are by the new birth made the children of grace.

Q20 *What is required of persons to be baptized?*
A   Repentance, by which they forsake sin, and faith, by which they firmly believe the promises of God proclaimed to them in that sacrament and through which, when they believe, they are accounted righteous before God solely on account of the merits of our Lord and Saviour Jesus Christ.

Q21 *Why then are infants baptized when by reason of their age they can neither repent nor believe?*
A   Because God has promised to be both our God and the God of our children. At baptism the parent(s) and

godparents of infants promise to bring them up in the Christian faith.

Q22   *Why was the sacrament of the Lord's Supper ordained?*
A   For the continual remembrance of the sacrifice of the death of Christ and of the benefits we receive from it.

Q23   *What is the outward part or sign of the Lord's Supper?*
A   Bread and wine, which the Lord has commanded us to receive.

Q24   *What is the inward part, or thing signified?*
A   The body and blood of Christ, which are truly taken and received, only in a heavenly and spiritual manner, by the faithful in the Lord's Supper.

Q25   *What benefits do we who partake receive?*
A   We are strengthened and refreshed in our souls by the body and blood of Christ, as our bodies are by the bread and wine.

Q26   *What is required of those who come to the Lord's Supper?*
A   They must examine themselves to see whether they truly repent of their sins and have resolved to lead a new life. They must have a living faith in God's mercy through Christ with a thankful remembrance of his death. And they must have love for all.

Confirmation

1   *The minister reads these words of* INTRODUCTION:

Our church requires that all who come to confirmation
should know and understand the Apostles' Creed, the
Lord's Prayer, and the Ten Commandments, and be
able to answer the other questions in the catechism.

When they come of age those baptized as infants may
openly take upon themselves and confirm, before the
people of God, the promises made in their name by
their godparents. They should seek the help and grace
of God to enable them to remain faithful to their
profession of faith. This we urge those who come now
to confirmation to do, praying that they would know
the Holy Spirit as their strength and guide as they serve
the Lord Jesus Christ.

2   *The bishop asks those who have come to confirmation:*

Do you here in the presence of God and this
congregation renew the solemn promises made in your
name at your baptism? Do you confirm that you repent
of your sins and renounce evil; that you sincerely
believe and trust in Christ; and that you will faithfully
obey God all the days of your life?

Answer   **I do.**

Bishop   Let us pray that God will strengthen with his Holy
Spirit these persons who now confirm their

commitment to those promises made at their baptism
and that they will serve Christ the Lord faithfully all
their days.

Our help is in the name of the Lord,

All **who has made heaven and earth.**

Bishop Blessed be the name of the Lord

All **now and for evermore.**

Bishop Lord, hear our prayer,

All **and let our cry come to you.**

3   *The bishop continues in prayer:*

Almighty and everliving God,
by whose grace these your servants
have been born again of water and the Spirit
and have received forgiveness of all their sins:
strengthen them with the Holy Spirit the Comforter;
daily increase in them your gifts of grace;
the spirit of wisdom and understanding,
the spirit of guidance and strength,
the spirit of knowledge and true godliness,
and fill them, O Lord, with the spirit of your holy fear,
both now and for ever. **Amen.**

4   *Those who have come to confirmation kneel before the bishop. He*
lays his hand upon the head of each and prays:

Defend, O Lord, your servant *N*
with your heavenly grace,
that *he* may continue yours for ever;
and daily increase in your Holy Spirit
until *he* comes to your eternal kingdom. **Amen.**

5   *Then the bishop says:*

The Lord be with you.
All   **And with your spirit.**
Bishop   Let us pray.

6   THE LORD'S PRAYER:

          either   *or*

All   **Our Father who art in**   **Our Father in heaven,**
             heaven,   **hallowed be your name,**
          hallowed be thy name,   **your kingdom come,**
          thy kingdom come,   **your will be done,**
          thy will be done,   **on earth as it is in heaven.**
          on earth as it is in heaven.   **Give us today**
          Give us this day   **our daily bread.**
          our daily bread.   **Forgive us our sins**
          And forgive us our   **as we forgive those**
             trespasses   **who sin against us.**
          as we forgive those   **Lead us not into**
             who trespass against us.   **temptation**
          And lead us not into   **but deliver us from evil.**
             temptation   **For yours is the kingdom,**
          but deliver us from evil.   **the power, and the glory,**
          For thine is the kingdom,   **now and for ever. Amen.**
          the power, and the glory,
          for ever and ever. Amen.

7   *The bishop continues in prayer:*

Almighty and everliving God,
you teach us both to intend and to do those things
that are good and acceptable in your sight.
We humbly pray for these your servants

upon whom we have laid our hands,
following the example of your holy apostles.
Reassure them of your favour and goodness;
let your fatherly hand always be over them;
may your Holy Spirit be ever with them;
lead them into all truth;
and teach them to obey your Word
so that in the end they obtain eternal life;
through Jesus Christ our Lord. **Amen.**

8

All **Almighty and everlasting God,**
be pleased, we pray,
to direct, sanctify,
and govern our hearts and bodies
so that we will keep your laws
and obey your commands;
and grant that through your mighty protection
we may be preserved in body and soul,
both here and for ever,
through our Lord and Saviour Jesus Christ. Amen.

9 *The bishop prays for those who have come to confirmation:*

The blessing of God Almighty, the Father, the Son, and
the Holy Spirit, be upon you, and remain with you for
ever. **Amen.**

*No persons shall be admitted to the Holy Communion until they
have been confirmed, or have been prepared for confirmation and
wish to be confirmed.*

153

Marriage

1   A HYMN *may be sung.*

2   *All sit, as the minister reads the* INTRODUCTION:

We have gathered here in the sight of God, and in the presence of this congregation to witness the joining together of *N* and *N* in marriage.

Marriage is an honourable state instituted by God in the time of man's innocence and signifies the union of Christ with his church. The Lord Jesus honoured a marriage at Cana in Galilee with his presence and there performed his first miracle. The Bible teaches that marriage is to be respected by all. It must not be entered into lightly or merely to satisfy physical desire, but with prayer, careful thought, and reverence for God, duly considering the purposes for which marriage was ordained.

First, marriage was established for the mutual companionship, help, and comfort that husband and wife should provide for one another both in prosperity and adversity. Secondly, it was established in order that the natural instincts and affections, implanted by God, should be hallowed and directed aright. Thirdly, marriage was established for the procreation of children, who should be brought up in the fear and nurture of the Lord and to the praise of his holy name.

It is into this holy state that *N* and *N* come now to be joined. Therefore if anyone can show any good reason why they may not be lawfully joined together, let him now speak or for ever remain silent.

3   *The minister says to the couple:*

N and *N*, I charge you both, as you will answer before God on the day of judgement, when the secrets of all our hearts shall be disclosed, that if either of you knows any reason why you may not lawfully be joined together in marriage, you must now confess it. For be assured, those who marry contrary to what God's Word allows are not joined together by God nor is their marriage lawful.

4   *The minister asks the groom:*

N, will you take *N* as your wife and live together as God has ordained? Will you love her, comfort her, honour and protect her, in sickness and in health; and, forsaking all others, be faithful to her as long as you both shall live?

Groom   **I will.**

5   *The minister asks the bride:*

N, will you take *N* as your husband and live together as God has ordained? Will you love him, obey him, honour and protect him, in sickness and in health; and, forsaking all others, be faithful to him as long as you both shall live?

Bride   **I will.**

6

Minister   Who gives this woman to be married to this man?

The minister receives the bride's right hand from her father, or friend, and passes it to the bridegroom.

7   *All stand to witness the marriage vows.*

8   *The bridegroom, taking the bride's right hand in his right hand, says:*

I *N* take you *N* to be my wife,
to have and to hold
from this day forward,
for better for worse,
for richer for poorer,
in sickness and in health,
to love and to cherish,
till death us do part,
according to God's holy law,
and this is my solemn vow.

9   *They loose hands and the bride, taking the groom's right hand in her right hand, says:*

I *N* take you *N* to be my husband,
to have and to hold
from this day forward,
for better for worse,
for richer for poorer,
in sickness and in health,
to love, cherish, and obey,
till death us do part,

according to God's holy law,
and this is my solemn vow.

10   *They again loose hands. A ring is placed upon a book. The*
      minister gives it to the groom who places it on the fourth finger
      of the bride's left hand. Holding it he repeats the following words
      after the minister (if the bride gives a ring the procedure may be
      repeated):

      I give you this ring
      as a sign of our marriage.
      With my body I honour you,
      all that I am I give to you,
      and all that I have I share with you:
      in the name of the Father,
      and of the Son,
      and of the Holy Spirit. **Amen.**

11   *The couple kneel, and the minister prays for them:*

      Eternal God, Creator and preserver of all mankind,
      giver of all spiritual grace, author of eternal life, send
      your blessing upon N and N so that, living faithfully
      together in love and peace, they may fulfil and keep
      the vow and covenant they have made, of which *these*
      rings are a token and pledge through Jesus Christ our
      Lord. **Amen.**

12   *The minister pronounces the couple to be man and wife. Joining*
      their right hands together he says:

      Those whom God has joined together let no one put
      asunder.

He then speaks to the people saying:

N and N have consented together in marriage and have witnessed the same before God and this congregation. They have made their vows to one another and have declared their marriage by the giving and receiving of *rings* and by the joining of hands. I therefore pronounce that they are husband and wife together in the name of the Father, and of the Son, and of the Holy Spirit. **Amen.**

13   *The minister blesses the newly married couple:*

God the Father, God the Son, God the Holy Spirit, bless, preserve, and keep you; the Lord mercifully with his favour look upon you and fill you with all spiritual blessing and grace that you may so live together in this life that in the world to come you may have eternal life. **Amen.**

14   THE BIBLE READING *and* SERMON

15   A HYMN *may be sung.*

16 THE LORD'S PRAYER:

either

All
Our Father who art in
heaven,
hallowed be thy name,
thy kingdom come,
thy will be done,
on earth as it is in heaven.
Give us this day
our daily bread.
And forgive us our
trespasses
as we forgive those
who trespass against us.
And lead us not into
temptation
but deliver us from evil.
For thine is the kingdom,
the power, and the glory,
for ever and ever. Amen.

or

Our Father in heaven,
hallowed be your name,
your kingdom come,
your will be done,
on earth as it is in heaven.
Give us today
our daily bread.
Forgive us our sins
as we forgive those
who sin against us.
Lead us not into
temptation
but deliver us from evil.
For yours is the kingdom,
the power, and the glory,
now and for ever. Amen.

17 *The minister leads the congregation in prayer using these or other*
PRAYERS:

God of Abraham, Isaac, and Jacob, bless *N* and *N* by
sowing the seed of eternal life in their hearts: so that
whatever they learn in your holy Word they may
indeed fulfil. Look on them from heaven and bless
them as you blessed Abraham and Sarah of old so that,
obeying your will and secure in your protection, they
may remain in your love to the end of their lives
through Jesus Christ our Lord. **Amen.**

Merciful Lord and heavenly Father, by your gracious
gift mankind is increased. Give to *N* and *N* the blessing
of children and grant them wisdom, grace, and health
to bring their children up in faith and goodness
to your praise and glory through Jesus Christ our
Lord. **Amen.**

Almighty God, you have consecrated marriage as a sign
of the union between Christ and his church. In your
mercy grant that *N* may love and cherish his wife as
Christ loves the church and that *N* may be loving and
submit to her husband as the church does to Christ.
Grant that in their marriage they may learn more of
your love and inherit your eternal kingdom through
Jesus Christ our Lord. **Amen.**

18   *The minister pronounces the final* BLESSING.

19   *The registers are signed.*

Burial (or Cremation) of the Dead

1   *The minister says these* SCRIPTURE VERSES:

I am the resurrection and the life, says the Lord. He who believes in me, though he dies, yet shall he live, and whoever lives and believes in me will never die. *John 11: 25–26 (RSV)*

I know that my Redeemer lives, and that in the end he will stand upon the earth. And after my skin has been destroyed in my flesh I will see God; I myself will see him with my own eyes. *Job 19: 25–27*

We brought nothing into the world, and we take nothing out of it. *1 Timothy 6: 7*

The Lord gave and the Lord has taken away; may the name of the Lord be praised. *Job 1: 21*

The eternal God is your refuge, and underneath are the everlasting arms. *Deuteronomy 33: 27*

2   A HYMN *or* A PSALM *may be said or sung by all:*

either   PSALM 23

**The Lord is my shepherd,
I shall not be in want.**

He makes me lie down in green pastures,
he leads me beside quiet waters,
he restores my soul.

He guides me in paths of righteousness
for his name's sake.

Even though I walk
through the valley of the shadow of death,
I will fear no evil,
for you are with me,
your rod and your staff,
they comfort me.

You prepare a table before me
in the presence of my enemies.
You anoint my head with oil;
my cup overflows.

Surely goodness and love will follow me
all the days of my life,
and I will dwell in the house of the Lord for ever.

or   *PSALM 90 (verses 1–6 and 11–12)*

Lord, you have been our dwelling-place
throughout all generations.
Before the mountains were born
or you brought forth the earth and the world
from everlasting to everlasting you are God.

You turn men back to dust, saying,
'Return to dust, O sons of men.'
For a thousand years in your sight

are like a day that has just gone by,
or like a watch in the night.

You sweep men away in the sleep of death;
they are like the new grass of the morning—
though in the morning it springs up new,
by evening it is dry and withered.

Who knows the power of your anger?
For your wrath is as great
as the fear that is due to you.
Teach us to number our days aright,
that we may gain a heart of wisdom.

3   THE BIBLE READING *follows. One of the following passages may
be read:*

John 14: 1–6

Jesus said: 'Do not let your hearts be troubled. Trust in
God; trust also in me. In my Father's house there are
many places of rest; if it were not so I would have told
you. I am going there to prepare a place for you. And if
I go and prepare a place for you, I will come back and
take you to be with me that you also may be where I
am. You know the way to the place where I am going.'

Thomas said to him, 'Lord, we don't know where you
are going, so how can we know the way?'

Jesus answered, 'I am the way, the truth, and the life.
No one comes to the Father except through me.'

1 Corinthians 15: 20–26, 35–38, 42–44, 50–58

Christ has been raised from the dead, the firstfruits of those who have fallen asleep. For since death came through a man, the resurrection of the dead comes also through a man. For as in Adam all die, so in Christ all will be made alive. But each in his own turn: Christ, the firstfruits; then, when he comes, those who belong to him. Then the end will come, when he hands over the kingdom to God the Father after he has destroyed all dominion, authority, and power. For he must reign until he has put all his enemies under his feet. The last enemy to be destroyed is death.

But someone may ask, 'How are the dead raised? With what kind of body will they come?' How foolish! What you sow does not come to life unless it dies. When you sow, you do not plant the body that will be, but just a seed, perhaps of wheat or something else. But God gives it a body as he has determined, and to each kind of seed he gives its own body.

So will it be with the resurrection of the dead. The body that is sown is perishable, it is raised imperishable; it is sown in dishonour, it is raised in glory; it is sown in weakness, it is raised in power; it is sown a natural body, it is raised a spiritual body.

I declare to you, brothers, that flesh and blood cannot inherit the kingdom of God, nor does the perishable inherit the imperishable. Listen, I tell you a mystery: we will not all sleep, but we will all be changed—in a flash, in the twinkling of an eye, at the last trumpet. For the trumpet will sound, the dead will be raised imperishable, and we will be changed. For the perishable must clothe itself with the imperishable, and the mortal with immortality. When the perishable has been clothed with the imperishable, and the mortal with immortality, then the saying that is written will come true: 'Death has been swallowed up in victory.'

'Where, O death, is your victory?

Where, O death, is your sting?'

The sting of death is sin, and the power of sin is the law. But thanks be to God! He gives us the victory through our Lord Jesus Christ.

Therefore, my dear brothers, stand firm. Let nothing move you. Always give yourselves fully to the work of the Lord, because you know that your labour in the Lord is not in vain.

1 Thessalonians 4: 13–18

Brothers, we do not want you to be ignorant about those who fall asleep, or to grieve like the rest of men, who have no hope. We believe that Jesus died and rose again and so we believe that God will bring with Jesus those who have fallen asleep in him. According to the Lord's own word, we tell you that we who are still alive, who are left till the coming of the Lord, will certainly not precede those who have fallen asleep. For the Lord himself will come down from heaven, with a loud command, with the voice of the archangel and with the trumpet call of God, and the dead in Christ will rise first. After that, we who are still alive and are left will be caught up together with them in the clouds to meet the Lord in the air. And so we will be with the Lord for ever. Therefore encourage each other with these words.

4   THE SERMON *is preached.*

5   THE LORD'S PRAYER:

either   *or*

All   **Our Father who art in**   **Our Father in heaven,**
       heaven,   **hallowed be your name,**
       hallowed be thy name,   **your kingdom come,**
       thy kingdom come,   **your will be done,**
       thy will be done,   **on earth as it is in heaven.**
       on earth as it is in heaven.   **Give us today**
       Give us this day   **our daily bread.**
       our daily bread.   **Forgive us our sins**
       And forgive us our   **as we forgive those**
       trespasses   **who sin against us.**
       as we forgive those   **Lead us not into**
       who trespass against us.   **temptation**
       And lead us not into   **but deliver us from evil.**
       temptation   **For yours is the kingdom,**
       but deliver us from evil.   **the power, and the glory,**
       For thine is the kingdom,   **now and for ever. Amen.**
       the power, and the glory,
       for ever and ever. Amen.

6   *The minister leads the people in* **PRAYER** *using one or more of*
           these, or other, prayers:

Almighty God, we rejoice that the souls of those who
have died trusting in the Lord Jesus Christ live with
you in everlasting joy and happiness. We thank you for
the life of *N* and for all that you have given us through
him. And we thank you that in mercy you have
delivered *him* from the miseries of this sinful life. In your
great goodness, Lord, complete soon the number
of your chosen children and hasten the coming of your
kingdom so that, along with all who have departed
trusting in Christ, we may be made perfect in body and

soul in your eternal glory, through Jesus Christ our Lord. **Amen.**

Heavenly Father, who gave your Son Jesus Christ to suffering and death on the cross, and raised him to life in glory, grant to us and all who mourn a patient faith in time of darkness, and strengthen our hearts with the knowledge of your love, through Jesus Christ our Lord. **Amen.**

Merciful God, whose Son Jesus Christ is the resurrection and the life: raise us from the death of sin to the life of righteousness, so that when we depart this life we may be found trusting in Christ and thus receive your eternal blessing, through Jesus Christ our Lord. **Amen.**

7   A HYMN *may be sung.*

8   *If the Committal is to take place at a different time the minister may conclude the funeral in church with these* BIBLE VERSES *(Jude 24 f):*

To him who is able to keep you from falling and to present you before his glorious presence without fault and with great joy—to the only God our Saviour be glory, majesty, power, and authority, through Jesus Christ our Lord, before all ages, now and for evermore. **Amen.**

9 THE COMMITTAL

The minister reads these verses from PSALM 103 *(verses 8, 10, 13–18):*

The Lord is compassionate and gracious,
slow to anger, abounding in love.
He does not treat us as our sins deserve
or repay us according to our iniquities.
As a father has compassion on his children,
so the Lord has compassion on those who fear him;
for he knows how we are formed,
he remembers that we are dust.
As for man, his days are like grass,
he flourishes like a flower of the field;
the wind blows over it and it is gone,
and its place remembers it no more.
But from everlasting to everlasting
the Lord's love is with those who fear him,
and his righteousness with their children's children
—with those who keep his covenant
and remember to obey his commands.

10 *The minister says these words. Some, or all, of the words in brackets may be omitted:*

It has pleased Almighty God to take from this world the soul of *N* here departed. We now commit *his* body (to the grave; earth to earth, ashes to ashes, dust to dust) in the sure and certain hope of the resurrection to eternal life for all who trust in Christ, who will change our frail and mortal bodies to be like his glorious resurrection body, according to his mighty power by which he is able to transform all things.

11   *The minister reads a* BIBLE VERSE:

Blessed are the dead who die in the Lord from now on.
Yes, says the Spirit, they will rest from their labour.
Revelation 14: 13

Cast all your anxiety on God because he cares for you.
1 Peter 5: 7

12   *The minister concludes with the* GRACE:

The grace of our Lord Jesus Christ,
and the love of God,
and the fellowship of the Holy Spirit,
be with us all evermore. **Amen.**

Interment or Scattering of Ashes

1   *The minister reads these* SCRIPTURE VERSES:

I am convinced, says the apostle Paul, that neither death
nor life, neither angels nor demons, neither the present
nor the future, nor any powers, neither height nor
depth, nor anything else in all creation, will be able to
separate us from the love of God that is in Christ Jesus
our Lord. *Romans 8: 38–39*

2   PSALM 121 *is said by all:*

I lift up my eyes to the hills—
where does my help come from?

My help comes from the Lord,
the maker of heaven and earth.

He will not let your foot slip—
he who watches over you will not slumber;
indeed, he who watches over Israel
will neither slumber nor sleep.

The Lord watches over you—
the Lord is your shade at your right hand;
the sun will not harm you by day,
nor the moon by night.

The Lord will keep you from all harm—
he will watch over your life;

**the Lord will watch over your coming and going
both now and evermore.**

3   *The minister says the words of* COMMITTAL:

Almighty God, our heavenly Father, we praise you for
the sure and certain hope of the resurrection to eternal
life for all who die trusting in the Lord Jesus Christ. We
now commit the ashes of *N* to the ground: earth to
earth, ashes to ashes, dust to dust; rejoicing that on the
last day Christ will transform the bodies of all who trust
in him into the likeness of his own glorious resurrection
body. **Amen.**

4   *The minister prays for the bereaved:*

Almighty God, Father of all mercies and giver of all
comfort, deal graciously, we pray, with those who
mourn, and especially with the family and friends of *N*
gathered here so that, casting all their care on you,
they may know the comfort of your love, through Jesus
Christ our Lord. **Amen.**

5   *Other prayers may follow, concluding with the* GRACE:

The grace of our Lord Jesus Christ,
and the love of God,
and the fellowship of the Holy Spirit,
be with us all evermore. **Amen.**

The Making of Deacons

1   *After* MORNING PRAYER *a* SERMON *is preached on the duty,
        office, and character of deacons.*

2   *The archdeacon (or his deputy) presents to the bishop those who
        are to be made deacons, saying:*

Reverend father in God, I present to you *these persons*
to be admitted as *deacons.*

The bishop says:

Have you made sure that the *persons* you present *are*
suited by *their* knowledge of Scripture and godly way
of life to exercise *their* ministry to the glory of God and
the good of his church?

The archdeacon:

I have enquired of *them*; *they have* been examined;
and I believe *them* fit for this office.

3   *The bishop addresses the people:*

Brothers and sisters, if any of you knows a reason why
any of these persons should not be made *a deacon,*
come forward in the name of God and make known
that reason.

If any objection is alleged against a candidate, the bishop shall postpone that candidate's ordination until he has satisfied himself that the objection alleged is without substance or may be properly disregarded.

4   *The bishop leads in* PRAYER. *The Litany (p. 52) is read and then the Holy Communion with this collect:*

Almighty God, by your divine providence you have appointed various orders of ministry in your church. Look in mercy on *these* your *servants* called to this office and responsibility, fill *them* with the truth of your doctrine and clothe *them* with holiness of life so that by word and example *they* may faithfully serve you in this office to the glory of your name and upbuilding of your church through the merits of our Saviour Jesus Christ, who lives and reigns with you and the Holy Spirit now and for ever. **Amen.**

5   *This* SCRIPTURE READING *from the Epistles is read:*

1 Timothy 3: 8–13 (RSV)

Deacons, likewise, must be serious, not double-tongued, not addicted to much wine, not greedy for gain; they must hold the mystery of the faith with a clear conscience. And let them also be tested first; then if they prove themselves blameless let them serve as deacons. The women likewise must be serious, no slanderers, but temperate, faithful in all things. Let deacons be the husband of one wife, and let them manage their children and their households well; for those who serve well as deacons gain a good

173

standing for themselves and also great confidence in the faith which is in Christ Jesus.

As an alternative Acts 6: 2–7 may be used.

6   *The bishop examines, before the people, those to be ordained:*

Bishop   Do you believe that you are led by the Holy Spirit to undertake this office and ministry, to serve God, for the promoting of his glory and the nurturing of his people?

Answer   **I believe so.**

Bishop   Do you think that you are truly called, according to the will of our Lord Jesus Christ, to the ministry of the church?

Answer   **I think so.**

Bishop   Do you sincerely believe all the canonical Scriptures of the Old and New Testament?

Answer   **I do believe them.**

Bishop   Will you diligently read them to the people assembled in the church where you are appointed to serve?

Answer   **I will.**

Bishop   The duties of deacons in the churches where they are appointed to serve are to assist presbyters in divine worship, especially at the administration of Holy Communion, to read the holy Scriptures, to instruct young people in the Christian faith as summarized in the catechism, to baptize when required to do so, and, if licensed by the bishop, to preach. In addition they are called to work with the members of Christ's church in caring for the sick and needy of the parish. Will you gladly and willingly do this?

Answer **I will, with God's help.**

Bishop Will you strive to live according to the teaching of Christ and teach your family to do the same so that you are good examples to the flock of Christ?

Answer **I will, with God's help.**

Bishop Will you reverently obey the ministers set over you in the church, gladly and joyfully following their godly advice?

Answer **I will, with God's help.**

7 *The bishop, laying his hands on each candidate, says:*

Take authority to carry out the office of a deacon in the church of God, now committed to you, in the name of the Father and of the Son and of the Holy Spirit. Amen.

The bishop, giving to each candidate a New Testament, says:

Take authority to read the Gospel in the church of God, and, if licensed by the bishop, to preach the same.

8 *This* SCRIPTURE READING *from the Gospels is read by one of them:*

Luke 12: 35–38

Be dressed ready for service and keep your lamps burning, like men waiting for their master to return from a wedding banquet, so that when he comes and knocks they can immediately open the door for him. It will be good for those servants whose master finds them watching when he comes. I tell you the truth, he will dress himself to serve, will have them recline at the table, and will come and wait on them. It will be good for those servants whose master finds them ready, even if he comes in the second or third watch of the night.

9 *The bishop proceeds with the* HOLY COMMUNION.

10 *After the last collect, and immediately before the blessing, these* PRAYERS *are said:*

Almighty God, giver of all good things, in your goodness you have been pleased to accept *these* your *servants* into the office of deacon in your church. Make *them*, we pray, O Lord, modest, humble, and faithful in *their* ministry, and ready to observe every spiritual discipline. May *they* always have the testimony of a clear conscience and enable *them* to remain stable and strong in your Son Jesus Christ, to whom be glory and honour now and for ever. **Amen.**

Go before us, O Lord, with your most gracious favour and further us with your continual help so that in all our works, begun, continued, and ended in you, we may glorify your holy name and at the end by your mercy obtain eternal life, through Jesus Christ our Lord. **Amen.**

11   *The bishop says this* BLESSING:

The peace of God which passes all understanding, keep
your hearts and minds in the knowledge and love of
God, and of his Son Jesus Christ our Lord; and the
blessing of God Almighty, the Father, the Son, and
the Holy Spirit, be upon you and remain with you
always. **Amen.**

The Ordination of Presbyters

commonly known as priests

1   *After* MORNING PRAYER *a* SERMON *is preached on the duty, office, and character of presbyters.*

2   *The archdeacon (or his deputy) presents to the bishop those who are to be ordained, saying:*

Reverend father in God, I present to you *these persons* to be ordained to the office of presbyter.

The bishop says:

Have you made sure that the *persons* you present *are* suited by *their* knowledge of Scripture and godly way of life to exercise *their* ministry to the honour of God and the good of his church?

The archdeacon:

I have enquired of *them; they have* been examined; and I believe *them* fit for this office.

3   *The bishop addresses the people:*

Good people, we purpose, God willing, to receive today *these persons* into the holy office of the presbyterate. After examination I find *they are* both fit for and called to this office and ministry. But if any of you knows a reason why *any of these persons* should not be received into this holy ministry, come forward in the name of God and make known that reason.

If any objection is alleged against a candidate, the bishop shall postpone that candidate's ordination until he has satisfied himself that the objection alleged is without substance or may be properly disregarded.

4   *The bishop leads in* PRAYER. *The Litany (p. 52) is read and then the Holy Communion, with this collect and the following Scripture readings:*

Almighty God, giver of all good things, by your Holy Spirit you have appointed various orders of ministry in your church. Look in mercy on *these* your *servants* now called to the presbyterate; fill *them* with the truth of your doctrine and clothe *them* with holiness of life, so that by word and example *they* may faithfully serve you in this office to the glory of your name and for the upbuilding of your church through the merits of our Saviour Jesus Christ, who lives and reigns with you and the Holy Spirit, now and for ever. **Amen.**

5   *These* SCRIPTURE READINGS *are read:*

Ephesians 4: 7–13

But to each one of us grace has been given as Christ apportioned it. This is why it says:
     'When he ascended on high he led captives
     in his train and gave gifts to men.'
(What does 'he ascended' mean except that he also descended to the lower, earthly regions? He who

descended is the very one who ascended higher than all the heavens, in order to fill the whole universe.) It was he who gave some to be apostles, some to be prophets, some to be evangelists, and some to be pastors and teachers, to prepare God's people for works of service, so that the body of Christ may be built up until we all reach unity in the faith and in the knowledge of the Son of God and become mature, attaining to the whole measure of the fullness of Christ.

and

either   *Matthew 9: 36–38*

When he saw the crowds, he had compassion on them, because they were harassed and helpless, like sheep without a shepherd. Then he said to his disciples, 'The harvest is plentiful but the workers are few. Ask the Lord of the harvest, therefore, to send out workers into his harvest field.'

or   *John 10: 1–16*

'I tell you the truth, the man who does not enter the sheep pen by the gate, but climbs in by some other way, is a thief and a robber. The man who enters by the gate is the shepherd of the sheep. The watchman opens the gate for him, and the sheep listen to his voice. He calls his own sheep by name and leads them out. When he has brought out all his own, he goes on ahead of them, and his sheep follow him because they know his voice. But they will never follow a stranger; in fact, they will run away from him because they do not recognize a stranger's voice.' Jesus used this figure of speech, but they did not understand what he was telling them.

Therefore Jesus said again, 'I tell you the truth, I am the gate for the sheep. All who ever came before me were thieves and robbers, but the sheep did not listen to them. I am the gate; whoever enters through me will be saved. He will come in and go out, and find pasture. The thief comes only to steal and kill and destroy; I have come that they may have life, and have it to the full.

I am the good shepherd. The good shepherd lays down his life for the sheep. The hired hand is not the shepherd who owns the sheep. So when he sees the wolf coming, he abandons the sheep and runs away. Then the wolf attacks the flock and scatters it. The man runs away because he is a hired hand and cares nothing for the sheep.

I am the good shepherd; I know my sheep and my sheep know me—just as the Father knows me and I know the Father—and I lay down my life for the sheep. I have other sheep that are not of this sheep pen. I must bring them also. They too will listen to my voice, and there shall be one flock and one shepherd.'

6   *The bishop addresses those to be ordained:*

You have heard, *brothers*, both beforehand in private and now in the sermon and Scripture readings, just how great and important is the office to which you have been called. I bid you in the name of our Lord Jesus Christ never to forget this and to remember what you are called to do. You are called to be *messengers, watchmen*, and *stewards* of the Lord. You are to teach and warn, to feed and nurture the Lord's family and to seek for Christ's sheep scattered abroad among the disobedient peoples of this world so that they may be eternally saved through Christ.

Have it always printed on your memory just how great a treasure is committed to your charge. The church and congregation whom you serve are Christ's spouse and body. They are his sheep, which he purchased with his death and for whom he shed his blood. You know what a great fault you will be guilty of if any member of his church is hurt or hindered as a result of your negligence and that God will discipline you. Therefore remember what God has called you to do. Never cease your careful and diligent labours until you have done all that you possibly can, according to your duty, to bring all those who are committed to your charge, to a knowledge of God, unity in the faith, and maturity in Christ so that no place is given to erroneous beliefs or wrong behaviour.

Since this office and ministry is both excellent and difficult, you will appreciate that you ought to be thankful to God for your call and that you need carefully to apply yourself to your duties and study. You must take care not to offend nor to cause others to sin. Only God can give you the desire and ability to do these things. You need therefore to pray earnestly for his Holy Spirit. And because there is no other way of leading men to salvation except by teaching the Holy Scriptures, you must read and learn them and order your *lives* and those of your *family* according to them. For the same reason you must forsake all those worldly cares and concerns that hinder you from doing your duty.

We are persuaded that you have carefully considered these things, and that you are clearly determined by God's grace to give *yourselves* wholeheartedly to this office and ministry to which God has been pleased to call you. Therefore continually pray to God the Father by the mediation of our only Saviour Jesus Christ for the heavenly assistance of the Holy Spirit so that through daily reading and meditation on the Scriptures, you will grow in your ministry, endeavour to sanctify and shape your *lives* and those of your *families* according to the rule and teaching of Christ, and be wholesome and godly *examples* for the people to follow. And now, so that the congregation of Christ's people gathered here may be assured of your determination to do these things and so that your public commitment to them may strengthen your resolve to do your duty, you shall plainly answer these questions which I, in the name of God and his church, now put to you:

Bishop   Do you believe that you are truly called, according to the will of our Lord Jesus Christ and the order of the Church of England, to the order and ministry of presbyter?

Answer   **I do.**

Bishop   Are you persuaded that the holy Scriptures contain all doctrine that is necessary for eternal salvation through faith in Jesus Christ? And are you determined to teach the people committed to your charge from those Scriptures, and to teach nothing as required or necessary for eternal salvation except that which you are persuaded can be proved by the Scriptures?

Answer   **I am persuaded, and will do so, by God's grace.**

Bishop   Will you carefully and faithfully minister the doctrine and sacraments, and the discipline of Christ, as the Lord has commanded, and as this church has received them, according to the commandments of God? And will you teach the people committed to your care to keep and observe them carefully?

Answer **I will, with the Lord's help.**

Bishop Will you be ready and careful to banish and drive away all wrong and strange doctrines that are contrary to God's Word and will you do this by means of public and private warning and exhortation, to the sick no less than to the well, whenever necessity requires it?

Answer **I will, with the Lord's help.**

Bishop Will you be diligent in prayer, in the reading of the holy Scriptures, and in those studies that help you to a fuller knowledge of them, turning away from worldly and unworthy concerns?

Answer **I will, with the Lord's help.**

Bishop Will you strive to live according to the teaching of Christ so that you and your *family* will be good examples to the flock of Christ?

Answer **I will, with the Lord's help.**

Bishop Will you maintain and promote to the best of your ability quietness, peace, and love among all Christians, but especially among those committed to your charge?

Answer **I will, with the Lord's help.**

Bishop Will you reverently obey those over you in the church, gladly and willingly accepting their godly counsel?

Answer **I will, with the Lord's help.**

7 *The bishop stands and says:*

Almighty God, who has given you the will to do all these things, grant you strength and power to perform them so that he may complete the work which he has begun in you through Jesus Christ our Lord. **Amen.**

8 *A short period of silence is kept during which the congregation PRAY for those to be ordained.*

9 *The candidates kneel, and this hymn* COME, HOLY GHOST *(Veni Creator Spiritus), or another suitable hymn, is sung.*

Come, Holy Ghost, our souls inspire,
and lighten with celestial fire;
thou the anointing Spirit art,
who dost thy sevenfold gifts impart.

Thy blessed unction from above
is comfort, life, and fire of love;
enable with perpetual light
the dullness of our blinded sight.

Anoint and cheer our soiled face
with the abundance of thy grace;
keep far our foes, give peace at home:
where thou art guide no ill can come.

Teach us to know the Father, Son,
and thee, of both, to be but One;
that through the ages all along
this may be our endless song:

Praise to thy eternal merit,
Father, Son, and Holy Spirit.

10   *The bishop says:*

Let us pray.

Almighty God and heavenly Father, by your infinite
love and goodness you have given us your only
beloved Son Jesus Christ to be our redeemer and the
author of eternal life. After he had secured our
redemption he ascended into heaven and sent into the
world his apostles, prophets, evangelists, teachers and
pastors, by whose ministry he gathered a great flock in
all parts of the world to proclaim the praise of your
holy name. For these great benefits, and because you
have called *these* your *servants* to the same office and
ministry appointed for the salvation of mankind, we
give you heartfelt thanks. We praise and worship you.
And we humbly pray that we and all who call upon
your name may be continually thankful for these and
all your benefits, that we may daily increase in faith
and the knowledge of you and your Son by the Holy
Spirit, and that through *these* your *ministers* and those
whom *they serve* your name may be ever glorified and
your kingdom enlarged, through your Son Jesus Christ
our Lord, who lives and reigns with you in the unity of
the Holy Spirit, world without end. **Amen.**

11   *The bishops and other ministers present lay their hands on the*
      head of each candidate, kneeling, and the bishop says:

Receive the Holy Spirit for the office and work of a
presbyter in the church of God, now committed to you
by the laying on of our hands. The sins you forgive,
they are forgiven; the sins you retain, they are retained.
And be a faithful minister of the word of God, and of
his holy sacraments in the name of the Father,
and of the Son, and of the Holy Spirit. **Amen.**

The bishop, giving to each candidate a Bible, says:

Take authority to preach the word of God, and to minister the holy sacraments in the congregation in which you are lawfully appointed.

12 *The* NICENE CREED *(p. 63 or p. 75) is said and the bishop proceeds with Holy Communion.*

13 *After Holy Communion and before the blessing these* PRAYERS *are said:*

Most merciful Father, we ask you to send upon *these* your *servants* your heavenly blessing. May *they* be clothed with righteousness and may your word spoken by *them* be so successful that it is never spoken in vain. Grant also that we may have grace to hear and receive the proclamation of your holy Word and that in all our words and deeds we may seek your glory and the increase of your kingdom, through Jesus Christ our Lord. **Amen.**

Go before us, O Lord, with your most gracious favour and further us with your continual help so that in all our works, begun, continued, and ended in you, we may glorify your holy name and at the end by your mercy obtain eternal life, through Jesus Christ our Lord. **Amen.**

14 *The bishop says this* BLESSING:

The peace of God which passes all understanding, keep your hearts and minds in the knowledge and love of God, and of his Son Jesus Christ our Lord; and the blessing of God Almighty, the Father, the Son, and the Holy Spirit, be upon you and remain with you always. **Amen.**

The Consecration of an Archbishop or a Bishop

1   *After* MORNING PRAYER *the Archbishop, or another Bishop, begins* HOLY COMMUNION *including this* COLLECT:

Almighty God, by your Son Jesus Christ you gave to your apostles many excellent gifts and commanded them to feed your flock. Give grace, we pray, to all Bishops, the pastors of your church, that they may diligently preach your Word and rightly teach your people from it, and grant that your people will obediently heed your Word so that all may receive the crown of eternal glory through Jesus Christ our Lord. **Amen.**

2   *The following* SCRIPTURE READINGS *are read by two other Bishops:*

either   *1 Timothy 3: 1–7 (RSV)*

The saying is sure: If any one aspires to the office of Bishop, he desires a noble task. Now a Bishop must be above reproach, the husband of one wife, temperate, sensible, dignified, hospitable, an apt teacher, no drunkard, not violent but gentle, not quarrelsome, and no lover of money. He must manage his own household well, keeping his children submissive and respectful in every way; for if a man does not know how to manage his own household, how can he care for God's church? He must not be a recent convert, or he may be puffed up with conceit and fall into the condemnation of the devil; moreover he must be well thought of by outsiders, or he may fall into reproach and the snare of the devil.

or   *Acts 20: 17–35*

From Miletus, Paul sent to Ephesus for the elders of the church. When they arrived, he said to them: 'You know how I lived the whole time with you, from the first day I came into the province of Asia. I served the Lord with great humility and with tears, although I was severely tested by the plots of the Jews. You know that I have not hesitated to preach anything that would be helpful to you but have taught you publicly and from house to house. I have declared to both Jews and Greeks that they must turn to God in repentance and have faith in our Lord Jesus.

And now, compelled by the Spirit, I am going to Jerusalem, not knowing what will happen to me there. I only know that in every city the Holy Spirit warns me that prison and hardships are facing me. However, I consider my life worth nothing to me, if only I may complete the task the Lord Jesus has given me—the task of testifying to the gospel of God's grace.

Now I know that none of you among whom I have gone about preaching the kingdom will ever see me again. Therefore, I declare to you today that I am innocent of the blood of all men. For I have not hesitated to proclaim to you the whole will of God. Keep watch over yourselves and all the flock of which the Holy Spirit has made you overseers. Be shepherds of the church of God, which he bought with his own blood. I know that after I leave, savage wolves will come among you and will not spare the flock. Even from your own number men will arise and distort the truth in order to draw away disciples after them. So be on your guard! Remember that for three years I never stopped warning each of you night and day with tears.

Now I commit you to God and to the word of his grace, which can build you up and give you an inheritance among all those who are sanctified. I have not coveted anyone's silver or gold or clothing. You yourselves know that these hands of mine have supplied my own needs and the needs of my companions. In everything I did, I showed you that by this kind of hard work we must help the weak, remembering the words the Lord Jesus himself said: "It is more blessed to give than to receive." '

and

either   *John 21: 15–17*

When they had finished eating, Jesus said to Simon Peter, 'Simon son of John, do you truly love me more than these?'

'Yes, Lord,' he said, 'you know that I love you.'

Jesus said, 'Feed my lambs.'

Again Jesus said, 'Simon son of John, do you truly love me?'

He answered, 'Yes, Lord, you know that I love you.'

Jesus said, 'Take care of my sheep.'

The third time he said to him, 'Simon son of John, do you love me?'

Peter was hurt because Jesus asked him the third time, 'Do you love me?' He said, 'Lord, you know all things; you know that I love you.'

Jesus said, 'Feed my sheep.'

or *John 20: 19–23*

On the evening of that first day of the week, when the disciples were together, with the doors locked for fear of the Jews, Jesus came and stood among them and said, 'Peace be with you!' After he said this, he showed them his hands and side. The disciples were overjoyed when they saw the Lord.

Again Jesus said, 'Peace be with you! As the Father has sent me, I am sending you.' And with that he breathed on them and said, 'Receive the Holy Spirit. If you forgive anyone his sins, they are forgiven; if you do not forgive them, they are not forgiven.'

or *Matthew 28: 18–20*

Then Jesus came to them and said, 'All authority in heaven and on earth has been given to me. Therefore go and make disciples of all nations, baptizing them in the name of the Father, and of the Son, and of the Holy Spirit, and teaching them to obey everything I have commanded you. And surely I will be with you always, to the very end of the age.'

3 *After the* NICENE CREED *(p. 63 or p. 75) and* SERMON *the Bishop-elect is presented by two other Bishops to the Archbishop of the province, who is seated in his chair near the holy table. These Bishops say:*

Most reverend father in God, we present to you *this* godly and learned *man* to be ordained and consecrated Bishop.

4 *The royal mandate is read, and this oath of obedience to the Archbishop is taken by each Bishop-elect:*

In the name of God, Amen. I *N*, chosen (suffragan/ assistant) Bishop of the church and see of *N*, do profess and promise all due reverence and obedience to the Archbishop and to the metropolitan church of *N* and to their successors: so help me God, through Jesus Christ.

5 *The Archbishop calls the congregation to prayer saying:*

It is written in the Gospel of Luke that our Saviour Christ spent a whole night in prayer before he chose and sent out his twelve apostles. It is also written in the book of Acts that the disciples at Antioch fasted and prayed before they laid hands on Paul and Barnabas and sent them out. Let us follow the example of Christ and the apostles and pray before we admit and send out *this person* presented to us to the work to which we believe the Holy Spirit has called *him*.

6 THE LITANY *(p. 52) is read.*

7 *The Archbishop says this* PRAYER:

Almighty God, giver of all good things, by your Holy Spirit you have appointed various orders of ministry in your church. Look in mercy on *this* your *servant* now called to the work and ministry of a Bishop. Fill *him* with the truth of your word and clothe *him* with holiness of life so that in word and deed *he* will faithfully serve you in this office to the glory of your name and the good of your church through the merits

of our Saviour Jesus Christ, who lives and reigns with
you and the Holy Spirit for ever and ever. **Amen.**

8　　　*The Archbishop, sitting in his chair, says to the Bishop(s)-elect:*

Brother, the holy Scripture and ancient canons
command that we are not to be hasty in laying on
hands and admitting anyone to government in the
church of Christ, which he has purchased at no less
price than the shedding of his blood. Therefore, before
I admit you to this ministry, I must examine you on
certain matters so that this congregation may know
how you will conduct yourself in the church of God.

Archbishop

Are you persuaded that you are truly called to this
ministry, according to the will of our Lord Jesus Christ,
and the order of the Church of England?

Answer　　**I am.**

Archbishop

Are you persuaded that the holy Scriptures contain
all doctrine that is necessary for eternal salvation
through faith in Jesus Christ? And are you determined
to teach the people committed to your charge from
those Scriptures, and to teach nothing as required or
necessary for eternal salvation except that which you
are persuaded can be proved by the Scripture?

Answer　　**I am persuaded and determined, by God's grace.**

Archbishop

Will you faithfully study the holy Scriptures and call on
God in prayer for the true understanding of them,
so that you will be able to teach and encourage with

193

wholesome doctrine and withstand and correct those
who contradict it?

Answer   **I will, with the Lord's help.**

Archbishop

Are you ready to banish and drive away all wrong
and strange doctrine that is contrary to God's Word
and will you both in public and private urge and
encourage others to do the same?

Answer   **I will, with the Lord's help.**

Archbishop

Will you turn away from all ungodly and selfish
desires and live a righteous and godly life so that by
your example the adversary may be put to shame and
have nothing to say against you?

Answer   **I will, with the Lord's help.**

Archbishop

Will you maintain and promote to the best of your
ability quietness, peace, and love among all men and
will you correct and discipline, according to the
authority of God's Word, the disorderly and
disobedient within your charge?

Answer   **I will, with the Lord's help.**

Archbishop

Will you be faithful in ordaining, commissioning,
and laying hands on others?

Answer   **I will, with the Lord's help.**

Archbishop

Will you be gentle and merciful for Christ's sake to
the poor, needy, and all strangers in need of help?

Answer   **I will, with the Lord's help.**

9   *The Archbishop stands and says:*

Almighty God, our heavenly Father, who has given you
the will to do all these things, grant you strength and
power to perform them so that he may complete the
work which he has begun in you through Jesus Christ
our Lord. **Amen.**

10   *This hymn* COME, HOLY GHOST (Veni Creator Spiritus), *or
another suitable hymn, is sung.*

Come, Holy Ghost, our souls inspire,
and lighten with celestial fire;
thou the anointing Spirit art,
who dost thy sevenfold gifts impart.

Thy blessed unction from above
is comfort, life, and fire of love;
enable with perpetual light
the dullness of our blinded sight.

Anoint and cheer our soiled face
with the abundance of thy grace;
keep far our foes, give peace at home:
where thou art guide no ill can come.

Teach us to know the Father, Son,
and thee, of both, to be but One;
that through the ages all along
this may be our endless song:

Praise to thy eternal merit,
Father, Son, and Holy Spirit.

11   *The Archbishop says:*

Let us pray.

Almighty God and heavenly Father, by your infinite
love and goodness you gave your only beloved Son
Jesus Christ to be our redeemer and the author of
eternal life. After he had secured our redemption and
ascended into heaven he poured down his gifts
abundantly on men, making some apostles, some
prophets, some evangelists, some teachers and pastors,
for the good and upbuilding of his church. Grant, we
pray, O Lord, to *this* your *servant* grace that *he* may be
always ready to proclaim your gospel, the good news of
reconciliation and salvation. Make *him a* wise and
faithful *steward* so that at the last *he is* received into
eternal joy through Jesus Christ our Lord, who lives
and reigns with you in the unity of the Holy Spirit,
world without end. **Amen.**

12   *The Archbishop and other Bishops present lay their hands on the*
       head of the Bishop-elect, kneeling, and the Archbishop says:

Receive the Holy Spirit for the office and work of a
Bishop in the church of God, now committed to you
by the laying on of our hands, in the name of the
Father and of the Son and of the Holy Spirit. Amen.
And remember to stir up the grace of God given you
by this laying on of our hands, for God has not given
us the spirit of fear, but of power and love and
self-control.

13   *The Archbishop gives the new Bishop a Bible, saying:*

Give yourself to reading, exhortation, and teaching.
Think on the things contained in this book. May what
you learn be evident to all. Apply these things carefully
to yourself and teach them to others, for in so doing
you will save yourself and those who hear you. Be to
the flock of Christ a shepherd, not a wolf; feed them,
do not devour them. Support the weak, heal the sick,
comfort the broken, restore the backslider, and seek the
lost. Be merciful and faithful in administering
discipline. And when the Chief Shepherd appears may
you receive the never-fading crown of glory through
Jesus Christ our Lord. **Amen.**

14   *After Holy Communion, and before the blessing, these* PRAYERS
are said:

Most merciful Father, we ask you to send upon *this*
your *servant* your heavenly blessing. Clothe *him* with
your Holy Spirit; enable *him* faithfully to preach your
holy Word; and make *him an example* of love, faith,
and holiness. Grant that *he* may fulfil *his* ministry and
that at the last *he* may receive the crown of
righteousness laid up by the Lord the righteous Judge,
who lives and reigns one God with the Father and the
Holy Spirit, now and for ever. **Amen.**

Go before us, Lord, with your most gracious favour
and further us with your continual help so that in all
our works, begun, continued, and ended in you, we
may glorify your holy name and at the end by your
mercy obtain eternal life, through Jesus Christ our
Lord. **Amen.**

15   *The Archbishop says this* BLESSING:

The peace of God which passes all understanding, keep
your hearts and minds in the knowledge and love of
God, and of his Son Jesus Christ our Lord; and the
blessing of God, Almighty, the Father, the Son, and
the Holy Spirit, be upon you and remain with you
always. **Amen.**

The Articles of Religion

Extracts from the Declaration of His Majesty King Charles I

. . . the Articles of the Church of England . . . do contain the true doctrine of the Church of England agreeable to God's Word . . . no man hereafter shall either print, or preach, to draw the Article aside any way, but shall submit to it in the plain and full meaning thereof: and shall not put his own sense or comment to the meaning of the Article, but shall take it in the literal and grammatical sense.

Canon A2 of the Church of England

The Thirty-Nine Articles are agreeable to the Word of God and may be assented unto with a good conscience by all members of the Church of England.

Canon A5 of the Church of England

The doctrine of the Church of England is grounded in the holy Scriptures, and in such teachings of the ancient Fathers and Councils of the Church as are agreeable to the said Scriptures. In particular such doctrine is to be found in the Thirty-Nine Articles of Religion, the Book of Common Prayer, and the Ordinal.

The Articles of Religion are set out below in their traditional form followed by a modern English equivalent or commentary. The latter is provided solely for the purpose of making the Articles more easily understood. The standing or authority of the Articles as set out in the Book of Common Prayer *is in no way to be interpreted as diminished or undermined.*

I   Of Faith in the Holy Trinity

There is but one living and true God, everlasting, without body, parts or passions; of infinite power, wisdom and goodness; the Maker, and Preserver of all things both visible and invisible. And in unity of this Godhead there be three Persons, of one substance, power, and eternity; the Father, the Son, and the Holy Ghost.

1   *Faith in the Holy Trinity*

There is only one living and true God, who is eternal and without body, indivisible and invulnerable. He is of infinite power, wisdom, and goodness. He is the maker and preserver of all things both visible and invisible. Within the unity of the Godhead there are three persons who are of one substance, power, and eternity—the Father, the Son, and the Holy Spirit.

II   Of the Word or Son of God, which was made very Man

The Son, which is the Word of the Father, begotten from everlasting of the Father, the very and eternal God, and of one substance with the Father, took Man's nature in the womb of the blessed Virgin, of her substance: so that two whole and perfect Natures, that is to say, the Godhead and Manhood, were joined together in one Person, never to be divided, whereof is one Christ, very God, and very Man; who truly suffered, was crucified, dead and buried, to reconcile his Father to us, and to be a sacrifice, not only for original guilt, but also for all actual sins of men.

2   *The Word, or Son of God, who became truly man*

The Son, who is the Word of the Father, was begotten from eternity of the Father, and is the true and eternal God, of one substance with the Father. He took man's nature in the womb of the blessed virgin Mary, of her substance, in such a way that two whole and perfect natures, the Godhead and manhood, were joined together in one person, never to be divided. Of these two natures is the one Christ, true God and true man. He truly suffered, was crucified, died, and was buried, to reconcile the Father to us and to be a sacrifice, not only for original guilt but also for all actual sins of men.

III   Of the going down of Christ into Hell

As Christ died for us, and was buried, so also it is to be believed, that he went down into Hell.

3   *The descent of Christ into the realm of the dead*

Just as Christ died for us and was buried, so also it is to be believed that he descended into the realm of the dead.

IV   Of the Resurrection of Christ

Christ did truly rise again from death, and took again his body, with flesh, bones, and all things appertaining to the perfection of Man's nature; wherewith he ascended into Heaven, and there sitteth, until he return to judge all Men at the last day.

4 *The resurrection of Christ*

Christ truly rose again from death and took again his body, with flesh, bones, and all that belongs to the completeness of man's nature. In this body he ascended into heaven, where he is now seated until the last day, when he will return to judge all men.

V Of the Holy Ghost

The Holy Ghost, proceeding from the Father and the Son, is of one substance, majesty, and glory, with the Father and the Son, very and eternal God.

5 *The Holy Spirit*

The Holy Spirit proceeds from the Father and the Son. He is of one substance, majesty, and glory with the Father and the Son, true and eternal God.

VI Of the Sufficiency of the holy Scriptures for Salvation

Holy Scripture containeth all things necessary to salvation: so that whatsoever is not read therein, nor may be proved thereby, is not to be required of any man, that it should be believed an article of the Faith, or be thought requisite or necessary to salvation. In the name of the holy Scripture we do understand those Canonical Books of the Old and New Testament, of whose authority was never any doubt in the Church.

Of the Names and Number of the Canonical Books.

Genesis
Exodus
Leviticus
Numbers
Deuteronomy
Joshua
Judges
Ruth
The First Book of Samuel
The Second Book of Samuel
The First Book of Kings
The Second Book of Kings
The First Book of Chronicles

The Second Book of
    Chronicles
The First Book of Esdras
The Second Book of Esdras
The Book of Esther
The Book of Job
The Psalms
The Proverbs
Ecclesiastes or Preacher
Cantica, or Songs of
    Solomon
Four Prophets the greater
Twelve Prophets the less

And the other Books (as *Hierome* saith) the Church doth read for example of life and instruction of manners; but yet doth not apply them to establish any doctrine; such are these following:

The Third Book of Esdras
The Fourth Book of Esdras
The Book of Tobias
The Book of Judith
The rest of the Book of Esther
The Book of Wisdom
Jesus the Son of Sirach
Baruch the Prophet

The Song of the Three
    Children
The Story of Susanna
Of Bel and the Dragon
The Prayer of Manasses
The First Book of Maccabees
The Second Book of
    Maccabees

All the Books of the New Testament, as they are commonly received, we do receive, and account them Canonical.

6   *The sufficiency of holy Scripture for salvation*

Holy Scripture contains all things necessary for salvation. Consequently whatever is not read in Scripture nor can be proved from Scripture cannot be demanded from any person to believe it as an article of the faith. Nor is any such thing to be thought necessary or required for salvation. By holy Scripture is meant those canonical books of the Old and New Testaments whose authority has never been doubted within the church.

The canonical books of the Old Testament are:

Genesis	1 Kings	Ecclesiastes	Obadiah
Exodus	2 Kings	Song of Songs	Jonah
Leviticus	1 Chronicles	Isaiah	Micah
Numbers	2 Chronicles	Jeremiah	Nahum
Deuteronomy	Ezra	Lamentations	Habakkuk
Joshua	Nehemiah	Ezekiel	Zephaniah
Judges	Esther	Daniel	Haggai
Ruth	Job	Hosea	Zechariah
1 Samuel	Psalms	Joel	Malachi
2 Samuel	Proverbs	Amos	

The canonical books of the New Testament are:

Matthew	2 Corinthians	1 Timothy	2 Peter
Mark	Galatians	2 Timothy	1 John
Luke	Ephesians	Titus	2 John
John	Philippians	Philemon	3 John
Acts	Colossians	Hebrews	Jude
Romans	1 Thessalonians	James	Revelation
1 Corinthians	2 Thessalonians	1 Peter	

The books of the Apocrypha, as Jerome *says, are read by the church for examples of life and instruction in behaviour,*

but the church does not use them to establish any doctrine.
They are:

1 Esdras	Baruch
2 Esdras	Song of the Three Children
Tobit	Susanna
Judith	Bel and the Dragon
Additions to Esther	Prayer of Manasses
Wisdom	1 Maccabees
Ecclesiasticus	2 Maccabees

VII   Of the Old Testament

The Old Testament is not contrary to the New: for both
in the Old and New Testament everlasting life is
offered to Mankind by Christ, who is the only
Mediator between God and Man, being both God and
Man. Wherefore they are not to be heard, which feign
that the old Fathers did look only for transitory
promises. Although the Law given from God by Moses,
as touching Ceremonies and Rites, do not bind
Christian men, nor the Civil precepts thereof ought of
necessity to be received in any commonwealth; yet
notwithstanding, no Christian man whatsoever is free
from the obedience of the Commandments which are
called Moral.

7   *The Old Testament*

The Old Testament is not contrary to the New, for in both
the Old and New Testaments eternal life is offered to
mankind through Christ. Hence he, being both God and
man, is the only mediator between God and man. Those
who pretend that the Patriarchs only looked for transitory
promises must not be listened to. Although the law given by
God through Moses is not binding on Christians as far as

its forms of worship and ritual are concerned and the civil
regulations are not binding on any nation state,
nevertheless no Christian is free to disobey those
commandments which may be classified as moral.

VIII   Of the Three Creeds

The Three Creeds, *Nicene* Creed, *Athanasius's* Creed,
and that which is commonly called the *Apostles'*
Creed, ought thoroughly to be received and believed:
for they may be proved by most certain warrants of
holy Scripture.

8   *The three Creeds*

The three creeds, the Nicene *Creed,* Athanasian *Creed, and*
that known as the Apostles' *Creed, ought to be*
wholeheartedly accepted and believed. This is because their
contents may be proved by definite statements of holy
Scripture.

IX   Of Original or Birth-sin

Original Sin standeth not in the following of *Adam*, (as
the *Pelagians* do vainly talk;) but it is the fault and
corruption of the Nature of every man, that naturally is
ingendered of the offspring of *Adam*; whereby man is
very far gone from original righteousness, and is of his
own nature inclined to evil, so that the flesh lusteth
always contrary to the spirit; and therefore in every
person born into this world, it deserveth God's wrath
and damnation. And this infection of nature doth
remain, yea in them that are regenerated; whereby the
lust of the flesh, called in the Greek, Φρόνημα σαρκὸς,
which some do expound the wisdom, some sensuality,

some the affection, some the desire, of the flesh, is not subject to the Law of God. And although there is no condemnation for them that believe and are baptized, yet the Apostle doth confess, that concupiscence and lust hath of itself the nature of sin.

9 *Original or Birth-sin*

Original sin is not found merely in the following of Adam's example (as the Pelagians foolishly say). It is rather to be seen in the fault and corruption which is found in the nature of every person who is naturally descended from Adam. The consequence of this is that man is far gone from his original state of righteousness. In his own nature he is predisposed to evil, the sinful nature in man always desiring to behave in a manner contrary to the Spirit. In every person born into this world there is found this predisposition which rightly deserves God's anger and condemnation. This infection within man's nature persists even within those who are regenerate. This desire of the sinful nature, which in Greek is called phronema sarkos *and is variously translated the wisdom or sensuality or affection or desire of the sinful nature, is not under the control of God's law. Although there is no condemnation for those that believe and are baptized, nevertheless the apostle states that any such desire is sinful.*

X Of Free-Will

The condition of Man after the fall of *Adam* is such, that he cannot turn and prepare himself, by his own natural strength and good works, to faith, and calling upon God: Wherefore we have no power to do good works pleasant and acceptable to God, without the grace of God by Christ preventing us, that we may have a good will, and working with us, when we have that good will.

10   *Free will*

The condition of man since the fall of Adam *is such that he cannot turn and prepare himself by his own natural strength and good works for faith and for calling upon the name of the Lord. Hence we have no power to do good works which are pleasing and acceptable to God, unless the grace of God through Christ goes before us so that we may have a good will, and continues to work with us after we are given that good will.*

XI   Of the Justification of Man

We are accounted righteous before God, only for the merit of our Lord and Saviour Jesus Christ by Faith, and not for our own works or deservings; Wherefore, that we are justified by Faith only is a most wholesome Doctrine, and very full of comfort, as more largely is expressed in the Homily of Justification.

11   *The justification of man*

We are accounted righteous before God solely on account of the merit of our Lord and Saviour Jesus Christ through faith and not on account of our own good works or of what we deserve. Consequently the teaching that we are justified by faith alone is a most wholesome and comforting doctrine. This is taught more fully in the homily on Justification.

XII   Of Good Works

Albeit that Good Works, which are the fruits of Faith, and follow after Justification, cannot put away our sins, and endure the severity of God's Judgement; yet are they pleasing and acceptable to God in Christ, and do spring out necessarily of a true and lively Faith; insomuch that by them a lively Faith may be as evidently known as a tree discerned by the fruit.

12   *Good works*

Although good works, which are the fruits of faith and follow on after justification, can never atone for our sins or face the strict justice of God's judgement, they are nevertheless pleasing and acceptable to God in Christ and necessarily spring from a true and living faith. Thus a living faith is as plainly known by its good works as a tree is known by its fruit.

XIII   Of Works before Justification

Works done before the grace of Christ, and the Inspiration of his Spirit, are not pleasant to God, forasmuch as they spring not of faith in Jesus Christ, neither do they make men meet to receive grace, or (as the School-authors say) deserve grace of congruity: yea rather, for that they are not done as God willed and commanded them to be done, we doubt not but they have the nature of sin.

13   *Works before justification*

Works done before receiving the grace of Christ and the inspiration of his Spirit are not pleasing to God. This is because they do not spring out of faith in Jesus Christ. Nor do they make people fit to receive grace or (as the schoolmen say) to deserve grace of congruity. On the contrary, because they are not done as God has willed and commanded that they should be done, it is undoubtedly the case that they have the nature of sin.

XIV   Of Works of Supererogation

Voluntary Works besides, over and above, God's Commandments, which they call Works of Supererogation, cannot be taught without arrogancy and impiety: for by them men do declare, that they do not only render unto God as much as they are bound to do, but that they do more for his sake, than of bounden duty is required: whereas Christ saith plainly, When ye have done all that are commanded to you, say, We are unprofitable servants.

14   *Works of supererogation*

The concept of voluntary works besides, over and above God's commandments, which are sometimes called works of supererogation, cannot be taught without arrogance and impiety. By them men declare not only that they render to God their proper duty but that they actually do more than their duty. But Christ says: 'So you also, when you have done everything you were told to do, should say, "We are unprofitable servants."'

XV   Of Christ alone without Sin

Christ in the truth of our nature was made like unto us in all things, sin only except, from which he was clearly void, both in his flesh, and in his spirit. He came to be the Lamb without spot, who, by sacrifice of himself once made, should take away the sins of the world, and sin, as Saint *John* saith, was not in him. But all we the rest, although baptized, and born again in

Christ, yet offend in many things; and if we say we have no sin, we deceive ourselves, and the truth is not in us.

15   *Christ alone is without sin*

Christ, who truly took our human nature, was made like us in every respect except that of sin. From this he was clearly free in both body and spirit. He came to be the Lamb without blemish who, by the sacrifice of himself once made, should take away the sins of the world. Sin, as St John says, was not in him. But all the rest of us, even though baptized and born again in Christ, still offend in many ways. If we say we have no sin, we deceive ourselves and the truth is not in us.

XVI   Of Sin after Baptism

Not every deadly sin willingly committed after Baptism is sin against the Holy Ghost, and unpardonable. Wherefore the grant of repentance is not to be denied to such as fall into sin after Baptism. After we have received the Holy Ghost, we may depart from grace given, and fall into sin, and by the grace of God we may arise again, and amend our lives. And therefore they are to be condemned, which say, they can no more sin as long as they live here, or deny the place of forgiveness to such as truly repent.

16   *Sin after baptism*

Not every sin knowingly committed after baptism is sin against the Holy Spirit and unforgivable. Therefore the gift of repentance is not to be declared impossible for those who fall into sin after baptism. After we have received the Holy Spirit we may depart from the grace given to us and fall into sin, and we may also by the grace of God return and amend our lives. Therefore those who say that they are incapable of sinning any more in this life are to be condemned, as are those who deny the opportunity of forgiveness to those who truly repent.

XVII   Of Predestination and Election

Predestination to Life is the everlasting purpose of God, whereby (before the foundations of the world were laid) he hath constantly decreed by his counsel secret to us, to deliver from curse and damnation those whom he hath chosen in Christ out of mankind, and to bring them by Christ to everlasting salvation, as vessels made to honour. Wherefore, they which be endued with so excellent a benefit of God be called according to God's purpose by his Spirit working in due season: they through Grace obey the calling: they be justified freely: they be made sons of God by adoption: they be made like the image of his only-begotten Son Jesus Christ: they walk religiously in good works, and at length, by God's mercy, they attain to everlasting felicity.

As the godly consideration of Predestination, and our Election in Christ, is full of sweet, pleasant, and unspeakable comfort to godly persons, and such as feel in themselves the working of the Spirit of Christ, mortifying the works of the flesh, and their earthly members, and drawing up their mind to high and heavenly things, as well because it doth greatly establish and confirm their faith of eternal Salvation to be enjoyed through Christ, as because it doth fervently kindle their love towards God: So, for curious and carnal persons, lacking the Spirit of Christ, to have continually before their eyes the sentence of God's

Predestination, is a most dangerous downfall, whereby the Devil doth thrust them either into desperation, or into wretchlessness of most unclean living, no less perilous than desperation.

Furthermore, we must receive God's promises in such wise, as they be generally set forth to us in holy Scripture: and, in our doings, that Will of God is to be followed, which we have expressly declared unto us in the Word of God.

17   *Predestination and election*

Predestination to life is the eternal purpose of God, whereby (before the foundations of the world were laid) he has consistently decreed by his counsel which is hidden from us to deliver from curse and damnation those whom he has chosen in Christ out of mankind and to bring them through Christ to eternal salvation as vessels made for honour. Hence those granted such an excellent benefit by God are called according to God's purpose by his Spirit working at the appropriate time. By grace they obey the calling; they are freely justified, are made sons of God by adoption, are made like the image of his only-begotten Son Jesus Christ, they walk faithfully in good works and at the last by God's mercy attain eternal happiness.

The reverent consideration of this subject of predestination and of our election in Christ is full of sweet, pleasant, and inexpressible comfort to the godly and to those who feel within themselves the working of the Spirit of Christ, putting to death the deeds of the sinful and earthly nature and lifting their minds up to high and heavenly things. This consideration establishes and confirms their belief in the eternal salvation to be enjoyed through Christ and kindles a fervent love towards God. But for inquisitive and unspiritual persons who lack the Spirit of Christ to have the sentence of

*God's predestination continually before their eyes is a
dangerous snare which the devil uses to drive them
either into desperation or into recklessly immoral living
(a state no less perilous than desperation).*

*Furthermore we need to receive God's promises in the
manner in which they are generally set out to us in holy
Scripture, and in our actions we need to follow that will
of God which is clearly declared to us in the Word of God.*

XVIII   Of obtaining eternal Salvation only by the Name of Christ

They also are to be had accursed that presume to say,
That every man shall be saved by the Law or Sect
which he professeth, so that he be diligent to frame his
life according to that Law, and the light of Nature. For
holy Scripture doth set out unto us only the Name of
Jesus Christ, whereby men must be saved.

18   *Obtaining salvation only by the name of Christ*

*Those who presume to say that every person shall be saved
by the rule of life, religion, or sect that he professes,
provided he makes diligent efforts to live by that rule and
the light of nature, must be regarded as accursed. For holy
Scripture declares to us that it is only in the name of Jesus
Christ that men must be saved.*

XIX   Of the Church

The visible Church of Christ is a congregation of
faithful men, in the which the pure Word of God is
preached, and the sacraments be duly ministered
according to Christ's ordinance in all those things that
of necessity are requisite to the same.

As the Church of *Jerusalem*, *Alexandria*, and *Antioch*,
have erred; so also the Church of *Rome* hath erred, not

only in their living and manner of Ceremonies, but also in matters of Faith.

19 *The church*

The visible church of Christ is a congregation of believers in which the pure Word of God is preached and in which the sacraments are rightly administered according to Christ's command in all those matters that are necessary for proper administration.

As the churches of Jerusalem, Alexandria, and Antioch have erred, so also the church of Rome has erred, not only in their practice and forms of worship but also in matters of faith.

XX Of the Authority of the Church

The Church hath power to decree Rites or Ceremonies, and authority in Controversies of Faith: And yet it is not lawful for the Church to ordain any thing that is contrary to God's Word written, neither may it so expound one place of Scripture, that it be repugnant to another. Wherefore, although the Church be a witness and a keeper of holy Writ, yet, as it ought not to decree any thing against the same, so besides the same ought it not to enforce any thing to be believed for necessity of Salvation.

20 *The authority of the church*

The church has authority to decree forms of worship and ceremonies and to decide in controversies concerning the faith. However, it is not lawful for the church to order anything contrary to God's written Word. Nor may it expound one passage of Scripture so that it contradicts another passage. So, although the church is a witness and guardian to holy Scripture, it must not decree anything contrary to Scripture, nor is it to enforce belief in anything additional to Scripture as essential to salvation.

XXI Of the Authority of General Councils

General Councils may not be gathered together without the commandment and will of Princes. And when they be gathered together, (forasmuch as they be an assembly of men, whereof all be not governed with the Spirit and Word of God,) they may err, and sometimes have erred, even in things pertaining unto God. Wherefore things ordained by them as necessary to salvation have neither strength nor authority, unless it may be declared that they be taken out of holy Scripture.

21 *The authority of general councils*

General councils may not be gathered together without the command and will of rulers. And when they are gathered together (since they are an assembly of men, among whom not all are ruled by the Holy Spirit and the Word of God), they may err. Indeed they sometimes have erred, even in things relating to God. Therefore anything commanded by them as necessary to salvation has no power or authority unless it can be shown to be taught by Scripture.

XXII Of Purgatory

The Romish Doctrine concerning Purgatory, Pardons, Worshipping and Adoration, as well of Images as of Reliques, and also invocation of Saints, is a fond thing vainly invented, and grounded upon no warranty of Scripture, but rather repugnant to the Word of God.

22   *Purgatory*

The Roman doctrine concerning purgatory, pardons, worshipping, and adoration (both of images and of relics), and the invocation of saints is a futile thing foolishly conceived and grounded on no evidence of Scripture. On the contrary this teaching is repugnant to the Word of God.

XXIII   Of Ministering in the Congregation

It is not lawful for any man to take upon him the office of publick preaching, or ministering the Sacraments in the Congregation, before he be lawfully called, and sent to execute the same. And those we ought to judge lawfully called and sent, which be chosen and called to this work by men who have publick authority given unto them in the Congregation, to call and send Ministers into the Lord's vineyard.

23   *Ministering in the congregation*

It is not right for any man to take upon himself the office of public preaching or of administering the sacraments in the congregation before he has been lawfully called and sent to perform these tasks. The lawfully called and sent are those who have been chosen and called to this work by men who have had public authority given to them in the congregation to call and send such ministers into the Lord's vineyard.

XXIV   Of speaking in the Congregation in such a Tongue as the people understandeth

It is a thing plainly repugnant to the Word of God, and the custom of the Primitive Church, to have publick Prayer in the Church, or to minister the Sacraments in a tongue not understood of the people.

24   *Speaking in the congregation in a language that people understand*

It is plainly repugnant to the Word of God and to the custom of the early church for public prayer or the administration of the sacraments to be conducted in a language not understood by the people.

XXV   Of the Sacraments

Sacraments ordained of Christ be not only badges or tokens of Christian men's profession, but rather they be certain sure witnesses, and effectual signs of grace, and God's good will towards us, by the which he doth work invisibly in us, and doth not only quicken, but also strengthen and confirm our Faith in him.

There are two Sacraments ordained of Christ our Lord in the Gospel, that is to say, Baptism, and the Supper of the Lord.

Those five commonly called Sacraments, that is to say, Confirmation, Penance, Orders, Matrimony, and extreme Unction, are not to be counted for Sacraments of the Gospel, being such as have grown partly of the corrupt following of the Apostles, partly are states of life allowed in the Scriptures; but yet have not like nature of Sacraments with Baptism, and the Lord's Supper, for that they have not any visible sign or ceremony ordained of God.

The Sacraments were not ordained of Christ to be gazed upon, or to be carried about, but that we should duly use them. And in such only as worthily receive the same they have a wholesome effect or operation: but they that receive them unworthily purchase to themselves damnation, as Saint *Paul* saith.

25   *The sacraments*

The sacraments instituted by Christ are not only badges or tokens of the profession of Christians but are also sure witnesses and effectual signs of God's grace and good will towards us. Through them he works invisibly within us, both bringing to life and also strengthening and confirming our faith in him.

There are two sacraments instituted by Christ our Lord in the Gospel—Baptism and the Lord's Supper.

The five that are commonly called sacraments (confirmation, penance, ordination, marriage, and extreme unction) are not to be regarded as Gospel sacraments. This is because they are either a corruption of apostolic practice or states of life as allowed in the Scriptures. They are not of the same nature as the sacraments of Baptism and the Lord's Supper since they do not have any visible sign or ceremony instituted by God.

The sacraments were not instituted by Christ to be gazed at or carried about but to be used properly. It is only in those who receive them worthily that they have a beneficial effect or operation. As Paul the apostle says, those who receive them in an unworthy manner bring condemnation upon themselves.

XXVI   Of the Unworthiness of the Ministers, which hinders not the effect of the Sacrament

Although in the visible Church the evil be ever mingled with the good, and sometimes the evil have chief authority in the Ministration of the Word and Sacraments, yet forasmuch as they do not the same in their own name, but in Christ's, and do minister by his commission and authority, we may use their Ministry, both in hearing the Word of God, and in the receiving of the Sacraments. Neither is the effect of Christ's ordinance taken away by their wickedness, nor the grace of God's gifts diminished from such as by faith and rightly do receive the Sacraments ministered unto them; which be effectual, because of Christ's institution and promise, although they be ministered by evil men.

Nevertheless, it appertaineth to the discipline of the Church, that inquiry be made of evil Ministers, and that they be accused by those that have knowledge of their offences; and finally being found guilty, by just judgement be deposed.

26   *The sacraments are not rendered ineffectual by the unworthiness of the minister*

Although in the visible church the evil are always mingled with the good and sometimes evil people possess the highest rank in the ministry of the Word and sacraments, nevertheless since they do not do these things in their own name but in Christ's and minister by his commission and authority, we may use their ministry both in hearing God's Word and in receiving the sacraments. The effect of Christ's institution is not taken away by the wickedness of these people, nor is the grace of God's gifts diminished, so long as the sacraments are received by faith and rightly. The sacraments are effectual because of Christ's institution and promise, even though they may be administered by evil men.

Nevertheless, it belongs to the discipline of the church that investigation be made into evil ministers. Those who are accused by witnesses having knowledge of their offences and who in the end are justly found guilty, should be deposed.

XXVII   Of Baptism

Baptism is not only a sign of profession, and mark of difference, whereby Christian men are discerned from others that be not christened, but it is also a sign of Regeneration or new Birth, whereby, as by an instrument, they that receive Baptism rightly are grafted into the Church; the promises of the forgiveness of sin, and of our adoption to be the sons of God by the Holy Ghost, are visibly signed and sealed; Faith is confirmed, and Grace increased by virtue of prayer unto God. The Baptism of young Children is in any wise to be retained in the Church, as most agreeable with the institution of Christ.

27   *Baptism*

Baptism is not only a sign of profession and a mark of difference by which Christians are distinguished from those who are not baptized. It is also a sign of regeneration or new birth, through which, as through an instrument, those who receive baptism in the right manner are grafted into the church, the promises of the forgiveness of sin and of our adoption as sons of God by the Holy Spirit are visibly signed and sealed, faith is confirmed, and grace is increased by virtue of prayer to God. The baptism of young children is undoubtedly to be retained in the church as that which agrees best with Christ's institution.

XXVIII   Of the Lord's Supper

The Supper of the Lord is not only a sign of the love that Christians ought to have among themselves one to another; but rather it is a Sacrament of our Redemption by Christ's death: insomuch that to such as rightly, worthily, and with faith, receive the same, the Bread which we break is a partaking of the Body of Christ; and likewise the Cup of Blessing is a partaking of the Blood of Christ.

Transubstantiation (or the change of the substance of Bread and Wine) in the Supper of the Lord, cannot be proved by holy Writ; but is repugnant to the plain words of Scripture, overthroweth the nature of a Sacrament, and hath given occasion to many superstitions.

The Body of Christ is given, taken, and eaten, in the Supper, only after an heavenly and spiritual manner. And the mean whereby the Body of Christ is received and eaten in the Supper is Faith.

The Sacrament of the Lord's Supper was not by Christ's ordinance reserved, carried about, lifted up, or worshipped.

28   *The Lord's Supper*

The Supper of the Lord is not only a sign of the mutual love that Christians ought to have among themselves. Rather, it is a sacrament of our redemption through Christ's death. To those who rightly, worthily, and with faith receive it, the bread which we break is a partaking of the body of Christ, and similarly the cup of blessing is a partaking of the blood of Christ.

Transubstantiation (the change of the substance of the bread and wine) in the Supper of the Lord cannot be proved from holy Scripture, but is repugnant to the plain teaching of Scripture. It overthrows the nature of a sacrament and has given rise to many superstitions.

The body of Christ is given, taken, and eaten in the Supper only in a heavenly and spiritual manner. The means by which the body of Christ is received and eaten in the Supper is faith.

The sacrament of the Lord's Supper was not instituted by Christ to be reserved, carried about, lifted up, or worshipped.

XXIX Of the Wicked which eat not the Body of Christ in the use of the Lord's Supper

The Wicked, and such as be void of a lively faith, although they do carnally and visibly press with their teeth (as Saint *Augustine* saith) the Sacrament of the Body and Blood of Christ, yet in no wise are they partakers of Christ: but rather, to their condemnation, do eat and drink the sign or Sacrament of so great a thing.

29 *The wicked who partake of the Lord's Supper do not eat the body of Christ*

The wicked and those who lack a living faith, although they physically and visibly 'press with their teeth' (as St Augustine says) the sacrament of the body and blood of Christ, nevertheless are in no way partakers of Christ. Rather, by eating and drinking the sign or sacrament of so great a thing, they bring condemnation upon themselves.

XXX Of both kinds

The Cup of the Lord is not to be denied to the Lay-people: for both the parts of the Lord's Sacrament, by Christ's ordinance and commandment, ought to be ministered to all Christian men alike.

30 *Reception in both kinds*

The cup of the Lord is not to be denied to the laity. For by Christ's institution and commandment both parts of the Lord's sacrament ought to be administered to all Christian people alike.

XXXI   Of the one Oblation of Christ finished upon the Cross

The Offering of Christ once made is that perfect redemption, propitiation, and satisfaction, for all the sins of the whole world, both original and actual; and there is none other satisfaction for sin, but that alone. Wherefore the sacrifices of Masses, in the which it was commonly said, that the Priest did offer Christ for the quick and the dead, to have remission of pain or guilt, were blasphemous fables, and dangerous deceits.

31   *The one oblation of Christ finished upon the cross*

The offering of Christ made once is the perfect redemption, propitiation, and satisfaction for all the sins of the whole world, both original and actual. There is no other satisfaction for sin but this alone. Consequently, the sacrifices of masses, in which it was commonly said that the priest offered Christ for the living and dead so as to gain remission of pain or guilt, were blasphemous fables and dangerous deceits.

XXXII   Of the Marriage of Priests

Bishops, Priests, and Deacons, are not commanded by God's Law, either to vow the estate of single life, or to abstain from marriage: therefore it is lawful also for them, as for all other Christian men, to marry at their own discretion, as they shall judge the same to serve better to godliness.

32   *The marriage of priests*

It is not commanded by any decree of God that bishops, presbyters, or deacons take a vow of celibacy or abstain from marriage. So it is lawful for them, as for all other

Christians, to marry at their own discretion when they judge that this will promote godliness.

XXXIII   Of excommunicate Persons, how they are to be avoided

That person which by open denunciation of the Church is rightly cut off from the unity of the Church, and excommunicated, ought to be taken of the whole multitude of the faithful, as an Heathen and Publican, until he be openly reconciled by penance, and received into the Church by a Judge that hath authority thereunto.

33   *The excommunicated: how they are to be avoided*

Any person who has openly been denounced by the church and justly cut off from its fellowship and excommunicated is to be regarded by the whole body of the faithful as a 'pagan and swindler' until he is openly reconciled by repentance and received back into the church by a judge who has the necessary authority in such matters.

XXXIV   Of the Traditions of the Church

It is not necessary that Traditions and Ceremonies be in all places one, or utterly like; for at all times they have been divers, and may be changed according to the diversities of countries, times, and men's manners, so that nothing be ordained against God's Word. Whosoever through his private judgement, willingly and purposely, doth openly break the traditions and ceremonies of the Church, which be not repugnant to the Word of God, and be ordained and approved by common authority, ought to be rebuked openly, (that others may fear to do the like,) as he that offendeth against the common order of the Church, and hurteth the authority of the Magistrate, and woundeth the consciences of the weak brethren.

Every particular or national Church hath authority to ordain, change, and abolish, ceremonies or rites of the Church ordained only by man's authority, so that all things be done to edifying.

34   *The customs of the church*

It is not necessary that customs and forms of worship be exactly the same everywhere. Throughout history they have differed. They may be altered according to the differing nations, times, and habits of people provided that nothing is commanded contrary to God's Word. Whoever by his own private judgement openly, willingly, and deliberately breaks those customs and forms of worship of the church which do not contradict the Word of God and are approved by common authority, is to be openly rebuked. This is so that others will be afraid to act similarly, and in so doing offend against the common order of the church, to undermine the authority of the state's representative and to wound the consciences of weak Christians.

Every particular or national church has authority to command, change, or abolish the ceremonies or forms of worship of the church which are appointed only by man's authority provided that everything is done for the building up of Christian people.

XXXV   Of Homilies

The second Book of Homilies, the several titles whereof we have joined under this Article, doth contain a godly and wholesome Doctrine, and necessary for these times, as doth the former book of Homilies, which were set forth in the time of *Edward* the Sixth; and therefore we judge them to be read in Churches by the Ministers, diligently and distinctly, that they may be understanded of the people.

Of the Names of the Homilies

1 *Of the right Use of the Church.*

2 *Against peril of Idolatry.*

3 *Of the repairing and keeping clean of Churches.*

4 *Of good Works: first of Fasting.*

5 *Against Gluttony and Drunkenness.*

6 *Against Excess of Apparel.*

7 *Of Prayer.*

8 *Of the Place and Time of Prayer.*

9 *That Common Prayers and Sacraments ought to be ministered in a known tongue.*

10 *Of the reverend*

estimation of God's Word.

11 *Of Alms-doing.*

12 *Of the Nativity of Christ.*

13 *Of the Passion of Christ.*

14 *Of the Resurrection of Christ.*

15 *Of the worthy receiving of the Sacrament of the Body and Blood of Christ.*

16 *Of the Gifts of the Holy Ghost.*

17 *For the Rogation-days.*

18 *Of the state of Matrimony.*

19 *Of Repentance.*

20 *Against Idleness.*

21 *Against Rebellion.*

35 *The Homilies*

The second Book of Homilies contains godly and wholesome teaching which is necessary for these times, as does the first book of Homilies published during the reign of Edward VI.

We therefore judge that they ought to be read diligently and distinctly in the churches by the ministers so that they may be understood by the people.

XXXVI   Of Consecration of Bishops and Ministers

The Book of Consecration of Archbishops and Bishops, and Ordering of Priests and Deacons, lately set forth in the time of *Edward* the Sixth, and confirmed at the same time by authority of Parliament, doth contain all things necessary to such Consecration and Ordering: neither hath it any thing, that of itself is superstitious and ungodly. And therefore whosoever are consecrated or ordered according to the Rites of that Book, since the second year of the forenamed King *Edward* unto this time, or hereafter shall be consecrated or ordered according to the same Rites; we decree all such to be rightly, orderly, and lawfully consecrated and ordered.

36   *The consecration of bishops and ministers*

The book for the consecration of archbishops and bishops and for ordaining presbyters and deacons, published in the time of Edward VI and confirmed at the same time by authority of Parliament, contains all things necessary to such consecration and ordination. Nor does it contain anything which of itself is superstitious and ungodly. Therefore whoever is consecrated or ordained according to the services of that book, since the second year of Edward VI to the present time, and whoever will be consecrated and ordained according to those services in the future, we declare to be rightly, duly, and lawfully consecrated and ordained.

XXXVII Of the Civil Magistrates

The King's Majesty hath the chief power in this Realm of *England*, and other his Dominions, unto whom the chief Government of all Estates of this Realm, whether they be Ecclesiastical or Civil, in all causes doth appertain, and is not, nor ought to be, subject to any foreign Jurisdiction.

Where we attribute to the King's Majesty the chief government, by which Titles we understand the minds of some slanderous folks to be offended; we give not to our Princes the ministering either of God's Word, or of the Sacraments, the which thing the Injunctions also lately set forth by *Elizabeth* our Queen do most plainly testify; but that only prerogative, which we see to have been given always to all godly Princes in holy Scriptures by God himself; that is, that they should rule all estates and degrees committed to their charge by God, whether they be Ecclesiastical or Temporal, and restrain with the civil sword the stubborn and evildoers.

The Bishop of *Rome* hath no jurisdiction in this Realm of *England*.

The Laws of the Realm may punish Christian men with death, for heinous and grievous offences.

It is lawful for Christian men, at the commandment of the Magistrate, to wear weapons, and serve in the wars.

37 *The state and its civil representatives*

The sovereign has the chief power in the realm of England *and his other possessions. The supreme government of all in this realm, whatever their station, whether ecclesiastical or civil, and in all matters, belongs to him and is not, nor ought to be, subject to any foreign jurisdiction.*

When we attribute to the sovereign the chief government (a title which seems to have offended some slanderous persons) we do not grant our rulers the ministry of either God's Word or of the sacraments. This is also made clear in the Injunctions published by Queen Elizabeth I. *By this title we acknowledge only the prerogative which we see in holy Scripture God has given to all godly rulers. They should rule all people committed to their charge by God, whatever their station or rank, whether ecclesiastical or secular, and restrain with the civil power those who are stubborn or practise evil.*

The bishop of Rome *has no jurisdiction in this realm of* England.

The laws of the realm may punish Christian people with death for heinous and grave offences.

It is lawful for Christian men at the command of the state to carry weapons and serve in wars.

XXXVIII Of Christian men's Goods, which are not common

The Riches and Goods of Christians are not common, as touching the right, title, and possession of the same as certain Anabaptists do falsely boast. Notwithstanding, every man ought, of such things as he possesseth, liberally to give alms to the poor, according to his ability.

38 *The possessions of Christians are not common to all*

Contrary to what some Anabaptists claim, the wealth and possessions of Christians are not common, as far as the right, title, and possession of them is concerned. Nevertheless, everyone ought to give freely to the poor from what he possesses, according to his means.

XXXIX   Of a Christian man's Oath

As we confess that vain and rash Swearing is forbidden Christian men by our Lord Jesus Christ, and *James* his Apostle, so we judge, that Christian Religion doth not prohibit, but that a man may swear when the Magistrate requireth, in a cause of faith and charity, so it be done according to the Prophet's teaching, in justice, judgement, and truth.

39   *A Christian's oath*

We believe that the vain and rash swearing of oaths is forbidden to Christians by our Lord Jesus Christ and St James. However, we judge that the Christian faith does not prohibit the swearing of an oath when the state requires it, if in a cause where faithfulness and love justify it, and according to the prophet Jeremiah's teaching, in justice, judgement, and truth.

Acknowledgements

Quotations from the Holy Bible (some in adapted form) in this publication are, unless otherwise stated, from the *New International Version (NIV)*, copyright © 1973, 1978, 1984 The International Bible Society. Anglicization copyright © 1979, 1986 Hodder & Stoughton Ltd.

Thanks are also expressed to the following for permission to reproduce copyright material:

The *Revised Standard Version (RSV)*, copyright 1946, 1952, © 1971, 1973 by the Division of Christian Education of the National Council of the Churches of Christ in the USA.

The Central Board of Finance of the Church of England, Prayers (some in adapted form), Canticles (*Easter Anthems, Song of Creation, Great and Wonderful, Saviour of the World*), and the Gloria from *The Alternative Service Book 1980* copyright © 1980 Central Board of Finance of the Church of England.

The text of the *Te Deum* is copyright © 1970, 1971, 1975 International Consultation on English Texts (ICET). The Lord's Prayer in its modern form is adapted from the ICET version.

The text of *Glory to God in the Highest (Gloria in Excelsis)* is from Latimer Monograph 3, copyright © 1972 Latimer House Council.

The pointing of the Canticles, Psalms 67, 95, 98, 100, the Songs of Mary, Simeon, and Zechariah, and *Gloria in Excelsis*, is by T. Hone, Organist of the Cathedral Church of St Nicholas, Newcastle upon Tyne.

ACKNOWLEDGEMENTS

The text of the Athanasian Creed is from *Confessing the Faith in the Church of England Today*, Latimer Study 9, copyright © 1981 Roger T. Beckwith.

The text of the *Song of Christ's Glory*, from the *South African Daily Office*, is copyright © The Church of the Province of South Africa.

This book contains material adapted from the *Book of Common Prayer* of 1662, rights in which are vested in the Crown, and which is used by permission of the Crown's patentee, Cambridge University Press.

Some of the prayers (pp. 39–48) are adapted from prayers in *Parish Prayers*, ed. Frank Colquhoun. New material copyright © Frank Colquhoun 1967, published by Hodder & Stoughton Ltd. Reprinted by permission.